THE GOSPEL OF JOHN

THE BRIDGE BIBLE TRANSLATION
Connecting the Biblical to the Contemporary World

© 2019 by Ryan Baltrip

All rights reserved. No part of this book may be reproduced in any form without permission in writing from the publisher, except in the case of brief quotations embodied in critical articles or reviews.

CONTENTS

JOHN CHAPTER 1 | page 1

1. **The Prologue: Recognize God's light (His revelation to the world) in Jesus Christ and God's gift of life (His way to redemption) through Him (1:1–18)**. 1

    1.1 Recognize that Jesus is God's Word (1:1–5).

    1.2 Recognize that God prepared the way for Christ (1:6–8).

    1.3 Recognize that the world is prone to reject Christ (1:9–11).

    1.4 Recognize that all who accept Christ will receive a new kind of life (1:12–13).

    1.5 Recognize that Jesus is the full revelation of God to the world (1:14–18).

2. **Discover Jesus and decide to follow Him (1:19–51)** 4

    2.1 Discover that Jesus is the Christ (He is coming, and He is here) (1:19–34).

        2.1.1 The newness of life is coming; Christ will bring it (1:19–28).

        2.1.2 The newness of life is here; the Spirit remains on Jesus (1:29–34).

    2.2 Decide to follow and learn from Jesus and discover a new kind of life (1:35–51).

        2.2.1 Decide to follow Jesus because of who He is (1:35–42).

        2.2.2 Decide to follow Jesus and discover what God will do (1:43–51).

JOHN CHAPTER 2 | page 10

3. **Jesus and the Jewish Institutions: Realize that Jesus reveals and establishes a new way to be right with God (2:1–4:54)**. 10

3.1 Unlike Jewish rituals, Jesus reveals He has the resources to meet people's needs, transform one's relationship with God, and infuse people with new life (2:1–12).

    3.1.1 A crisis develops around the lack of resources at a wedding, and Jesus is driven by God's mission for His life (2:1–4).

    3.1.2 The stone jars used in ritual cleansing lack the resources to meet people's needs (2:5–6).

    3.1.3 Jesus has the resources to meet people's needs and transforms the water into wine (2:7–8).

    3.1.4 Jesus transforms the situation and infuses it with new life (2:9–10).

    3.1.5 Jesus can transform one's relationship with God and infuse people with new life (2:11–12).

3.2 Unlike the Jewish temple, Jesus reveals that the center of God's plan revolves around His own person, mission, and work (2:13–25).

    3.2.1 The purpose of God's temple in the Old Covenant had been defiled (2:13–14).

    3.2.2 Jesus calls everyone to refocus on the temple's true purpose (2:15–17).

    3.2.3 The authority of Jesus is questioned, and He foreshadows the sign of a greater temple—His crucified and resurrected body (2:18–20).

    3.2.4 They fail to understand the greater Temple—Jesus' body (2:20–22).

    3.2.5 Jesus' teaching leads to a response (2:23–25).

JOHN CHAPTER 3 | page 15

3.3 Unlike Jewish rabbis, Jesus reveals a new way of belonging to God's kingdom and experiencing a new kind of life that eternally endures (3:1–21).

    3.3.1 A new way of belonging to God requires a new birth (3:1–8).

    3.3.2 A new way of belonging to God requires believing in Jesus Christ (3:9–18).

    3.3.3 A new way of belonging to God brings His light into life (3:19–21).

3.4 Unlike Jewish perspectives on baptism, Jesus is the focus of God's work in the world; all focus should be on Him (3:22–36).

    3.4.1 A question about baptism raises a bigger question: Where should the focus be in one's relationship with God? (3:22–26).

    3.4.2 Jesus Christ is the focus of God's work in the world (3:27–30).

    3.4.3 Jesus Christ should be the focus of one's life with God (3:31–36).

JOHN CHAPTER 4 | page 21

3.5 Unlike Jewish debates on where and how to worship God, Jesus reveals a new way to worship God; offers a new, eternal provision of a life in direct connection with God; and breaks down barriers between people (4:1–42).

- 3.5.1 Jesus provides a new way to worship God (4:1–26).
- 3.5.2 Jesus offers a new life of eternal provision from God (4:27–38).
- 3.5.3 Jesus breaks down barriers between people as they come to believe in Him (4:39–42).

3.6 Unlike the Jewish response, Jesus reveals that believing in Him is not about His miracles but about trusting in who He is—the Son of God (4:43–54).
- 3.6.1 Many people only look to God because of what they think He can do for them (4:43–45).
- 3.6.2 More than a miracle worker who meets needs, Jesus is the Son of God (4:46–54).

JOHN CHAPTER 5 | page 28

4. Jesus and Jewish festivals: Realize that Jesus defines a new way of life dedicated to God (5:1–10:42). 28

4.1 Jesus and the Festival of Sabbath: Jesus is the Son of God who has His power and authority over life and His ability to give life to others (5:1–47).
- 4.1.1 The alleged criminal activity: Jesus breaks the religious and cultural norm by healing and giving the gift of life on the Sabbath (5:1–15).
- 4.1.2 The Deliberation: Even though some people may be unsure, Jesus, as the Son of God, has the authority to give life any time He wants (5:16–30).
- 4.1.3 The Evidence for Jesus: All the evidence of God's work in the world shows that Jesus is the Son of God who will save the world (5:31–47).

JOHN CHAPTER 6 | page 36

4.2 Jesus and the Festival of Passover: Jesus is the Son of God who meets people's needs by providing for their ultimate salvation and by giving them the sustenance they need as they travel through life (6:1–71).
- 4.2.1 Christ feeds 5,000: Unlike the old way that did not fully meet peoples lasting needs, Jesus is the Christ who meets people's needs by providing ultimate deliverance and salvation to God's people (6:1–15).
- 4.2.2 Christ walks on water: Unlike the old water miracle that temporarily provided water from a rock, Jesus has power and authority over water itself (6:16–24).
- 4.2.3 Jesus is the bread of life: Unlike manna from heaven that temporarily met people's needs, Jesus is the source of life, the satisfaction of the human heart, and the goal of God's work in the world (6:25–59).
- 4.2.4 Responding to Jesus: Jesus' sacrificed body is the source of life and calls everyone to make a decision about Him (6:60–71).

JOHN CHAPTER 7 | page 46

    4.3   Jesus and the Festival of Tabernacles: Jesus is the Son of God who provides those who believe in Him with an internal source of life-giving water that will never end; He is the full light of God's revelation to the world (7:1—9:41)

        4.3.1   Jesus is the Christ who comes from the Father and has the authority to give life (7:1–52).

JOHN CHAPTER 8 | page 53

        4.3.2   While many—including religious leaders—may condemn one's sinful behaviors, Jesus offers forgiveness; He calls everyone to follow God's new way of life (7:53–8:11).

        4.3.3   Jesus is God's light—His revelation—that illuminates one's life and guides them through every aspect of life (8:12–30).

JOHN CHAPTER 9 | page 61

        4.3.4   Who is truly blind and who can really see? Jesus heals a blind man, showing His power and authority over life, and it reveals the spiritual blindness of those who do not believe in Him (9:1–41).

JOHN CHAPTER 10 | page 67

    4.4   **Jesus and the Festival of Hanukkah: Jesus is the Son of God who guides and leads God's people in the way of life (10:1-39).**

        4.4.1   Jesus is the gate through which people gain access to God's family, and He is the Good Shepherd who knows and leads His sheep (His people) (10:1–21).

        4.4.2   Jesus' claims to be the Christ, and people must make a decision about Him (10:22–39).

JOHN CHAPTER 11 | page 72

5.   Jesus reveals God's light to the world (how He will save His people), and everyone who comes to God's light will no longer live in darkness (11:1–12:50)..........................72

    5.1   Jesus demonstrates His power over life and death; yet, people plot to kill Jesus (not knowing they are actually fulfilling God's plan) (11:1–57).

        5.1.1   Jesus provides a paradigm for how God will save His people (11:1–44).

        5.1.2   Even though Jesus has demonstrated His power over life and death, people still refuse to believe in Jesus and plot to kill Him (11:45-57).

JOHN CHAPTER 12 | page 79

    5.2   Jesus is anointed for death (and His coming victory), and He enters Jerusalem to fulfill God's plan—offering people salvation through His death and resurrection (12:1–50).

5.2.1	Jesus is anointed by Mary for His death and coming victory (12:1–11).
5.2.2	Even though people celebrate Jesus' triumphal entry into Jerusalem like He's a military victor, Jesus demonstrates that His victory will be achieved as a sacrificial servant (12:12–19).
5.2.3	Jesus tells His disciples what is about to happen, but they do not fully understand it yet (12:20–36).
5.2.4	Sadly, too many people persist in their unbelief, having closed their eyes, minds, and hearts to Jesus (12:37–43).
5.2.5	Jesus makes one final public plea with the people He came to save, letting them know that those who believe will be saved and those who do not will be judged and condemned (12:44–50).

JOHN CHAPTER 13 | page 86

6. Believing in Jesus is just the starting point of a life with God; one must continue to trust in Him (13:1—17:26).......... 86

6.1 Jesus provides an example to follow (13:1–30).

6.1.1 Those who believe should follow Jesus's example and serve others (13:1–20).

6.1.2 Those who believe must persist in following Jesus' light because the darkness of the night is coming (13:21–30).

6.2 Jesus gives a teaching to follow (13:31–17:26).

JOHN CHAPTER 14 | page 91

6.2.1 Believers will be tested when Jesus departs this world, but He will provide for their needs when He is gone through the Holy Spirit (13:31–14:31).

JOHN CHAPTER 15 | page 95

6.2.2 Believers must remain vitally connected to the source of this new kind of life (15:1–17).

JOHN CHAPTER 16 | page 98

6.2.3 Believers will live and face challenges in the world, but the Holy Spirit will help them to thrive for God through it all (15:18–16:33).

JOHN CHAPTER 17 | page 103

6.2.4 Jesus prays for His disciples to reflect His character and to demonstrate His value and worth as they live in the world (17:1–26).

JOHN CHAPTER 18 | page 107

7. Jesus reveals God's path to redemption through His crucifixion, death, and resurrection (18:1–20:29). 107

7.1 Conviction: Jesus is arrested and shows that His way is not through military revolution but through sacrificial service and sharing the truth (18:1–19:16).

7.1.1 Jesus is arrested and shows that His way is not through a forceful revolt (18:1–11).

7.1.2 The religious leaders put Jesus on trial for claiming to be God; they convict Him of a crime punishable by death (18:12–27).

JOHN CHAPTER 19 | page 112

7.1.3 The Roman trial: Jesus is brought to stand trial before the Romans because they have the power to put Jesus to death for a capital offense. (18:28–19:16).

7.2 Crucifixion: Jesus, the Son of God, gives His life for the world (19:17–42).

7.2.1 Crucified: Jesus fulfills God's plan and is crucified on behalf of the world (19:17–27).

7.2.2 Death: Jesus fulfills God's plan and dies for the world's benefit (19:28–37).

7.2.3 Buried: Jesus fulfills God's plan and is buried in a tomb (19:38–42).

JOHN CHAPTER 20 | page 118

7.3 Resurrection: Jesus, the Son of God, gives a new kind of life to the world through His resurrection (20:1–29).

7.3.1 The empty tomb: Jesus has risen from the dead, overcoming death, the Devil, and a world living in darkness (20:1–10).

7.3.2 Jesus has risen from the dead, and the time is coming for Him to ascend to the Father in heaven (20:11–18).

7.3.3 Jesus has risen from the dead, and He brings peace to His followers, gives them the Holy Spirit, and sends them out into the world to continue God's work in it (20:19–23).

7.3.4 Jesus has risen from the dead, and He provides Thomas with the physical evidence of His resurrection so that he will believe; yet, Jesus says that those who believe without seeing Him physically are supernaturally blessed by God (20:24–29).

8. The Purpose of John's Gospel: Believe in Jesus and continue to believe in Him (20:30–31). 122

JOHN CHAPTER 21 | page 122

9. **The Conclusion of the Gospel of John: Believers will continue to live by faith in the resurrected Christ and continue His work in the world (21:1–25).** 122

    9.1   Even after the resurrection, Jesus provides for His followers and continues His work in the world through them (21:1–14).

    9.2   Believers may come short of what God wants for them, but Jesus restores them, and He refocuses them so that they can carry on His continuing work in the world (21:15–23).

    9.3   Much more could be said, but believers have this official, eye-witness account to encourage their belief in the truth of God revealed in Jesus Christ (21:24–25).

THE GOSPEL OF JOHN

1. The Prologue: Recognize God's light (His revelation to the world) in Jesus Christ and God's gift of life (His way to redemption) through Him (1:1–18).

   1.1 Recognize that Jesus is God's Word (1:1–5).

   CHAPTER 1

¹In the beginning, the Word already existed. Before human history began and before the world was created, the Word existed. The Word—God's personal and creative power at work in the world—existed in the person of Jesus Christ.

Jesus, the One who is the Word, has always shared eternity with God. Jesus, the Son, has always existed as distinct yet inseparable from the presence of God, the Father.

Jesus, the One who is the Word, was, is, and always will be fully God.

²Jesus was not an act of God's creation. Instead, He was present with God, the Father, at the beginning of creation.

³Through Jesus, God created everything. Nothing—not one thing in all of creation—was made without Him. Jesus is both the creative mediator of the universe and the unifying principle and purpose at the heart of all existence.

⁴Jesus is the source of all life. His life brought a general light of conscience and reason to all people. But His life also brought a specific, personal, and spiritual light that reveals God to the world He made. ⁵His light shines into the spiritual darkness and illuminates humanity. Even though this world lives in spiritual darkness and often fails to understand the light, the darkness of the world can never overpower God's light.

1.2 Recognize that God prepared the way for Christ (1:6–8).

⁶God sent a man into the world with a mission. His name was John the Baptist. ⁷His mission was to be a witness who could testify to God's truth. His goal was to tell all people about the illuminating light of life found in Jesus Christ. His aim was that all people might trust in Jesus. ⁸John the Baptist was not God's light, and he made sure everyone knew it. Instead, John the Baptist lived to lead others to God's light.

1.3 Recognize that the world is prone to reject Christ (1:9–11).

⁹The true light from God—Jesus, the One who illuminates everyone's conscience and reason and who also reveals God's ways by shining His light into darkness—was coming into the world. ¹⁰Jesus, the One who is the Word, came into the world He created. However, the world did not recognize Him as the source of all life and the central purpose of human existence. ¹¹Jesus came to His own people, the Jewish people of the Old Covenant [Old Testament]. God had been working many years to prepare them to receive Jesus. Yet when Jesus came to them, even they rejected Him.

1.4 Recognize that all who accept Christ will receive a new kind of life (1:12–13).

¹²But God did not send Jesus only to a specific group of people. Instead, God opened the doors for everyone to access the new life

He gives. To everyone who received Jesus—regardless of their societal rank, intelligence, age, gender, race, or background—He gave the power and authority to take on a new identity as part of a new family. To everyone who accepted Jesus' claims and dedicated their lives to following Him, He gave the right to become children of God, personally valued and loved members who belong to His family.

¹³They did not become children of God through any natural means—through passionate, human desire (like sexual desire) or intense, focused human initiative (like sexual initiative). Instead, they were born of God through His supernatural action.

1.5 Recognize that Jesus is the full revelation of God to the world (1:14–18)

¹⁴The Word—God's personal and creative working in the world—became flesh in the person of Jesus. In the flesh of Jesus, God made a temporary home among us as a human being living in our world. In the flesh of Jesus, God's glorious presence dwelt among us like a tabernacle of light shining in the dark wilderness of our world. While Jesus was dwelling among us, we saw His glory with our own eyes. We witnessed the glory of Jesus' entire life and ministry on earth, a glory that can only be embodied by God the Father's one and only Son. We learned that Jesus is the source and fullness of God's grace and truth.

¹⁵As the final voice preparing God's people for Jesus' arrival, John the Baptist provided a first-hand, eyewitness account to the grace and truth of Jesus. John called out to the crowds, "This is the One I was talking about when I said, 'Someone is coming after me who is far greater than I am because He is God and existed before I was born.'"

¹⁶Out of His fullness, we have all received a continuous flow of God's gracious gifts throughout our lives, with every new gift of grace arriving right after the other. ¹⁷We received a basic introduction to God's grace when He gave us His guidance in the Old Covenant Law, which God gave us through Moses. But Jesus Christ fulfills the Old Covenant's teachings and gives us an endlessly flowing relationship

with Him. Through Jesus Christ, we know the fullness of God's grace and truth.

¹⁸No one has ever seen God the Father except for Jesus. Jesus—the Son who is fully God Himself—is at the Father's side and is intimately close to His heart. Everything that God wanted us to know about Himself He has shown us through the person and work of Jesus.

THE BOOK OF SIGNS (1:19–12:50)

2. Discover Jesus and decide to follow Him (1:19–51)

2.1 Discover that Jesus is the Christ (He is coming, and He is here) (1:19–34).

2.1.1 The newness of life is coming; Christ will bring it (1:19–28).

¹⁹When John the Baptist was confronted by the Jewish leaders, he gave this testimony to the truth found in Jesus. John the Baptist had been baptizing people independent of Jewish authority. This was an unusual phenomenon that broke with their custom, so the Jewish religious leaders sent a delegation of priests and experts in the religious law to interrogate him. They interrogated John the Baptist about his identity and authority by asking him three different questions. First, they asked him, "Who are you? Are you the Messiah who is the Christ–the anointed One filled with God's power and authority who will decisively deliver God's people?"

²⁰John the Baptist did not want there to be any confusion on this matter, so he answered as clearly and as straight-forward as possible, saying, "I am not the Messiah."

²¹Second, they asked John, "Who are you then? We suspect Elijah, the prophet-leader mentioned in the Scriptures of 1 and 2 Kings, is still alive, and we believe that he will return at the end of time. Are you Elijah who has returned?" John replied, "No, I am not."

Third, they asked John, "We are also expecting a great prophet, the one that Moses predicted in Deuteronomy 18:15–19, who will usher in a fully righteous world. Are you this Great Prophet?" John replied, "No, I am not."

²²Having reached the end of their primary line of questioning, they were frustrated that they had not discovered anything. They asked, "We need some piece of information to take back to the religious leaders who sent us. What do you want us to tell them? Just tell us who you are and what your purpose is."

²³John answered by quoting Isaiah 40:3, saying, "I am the voice of one calling out in the wilderness, 'Prepare a straight path for the Lord's arrival because His arrival is at hand!'"

²⁴Then, some Pharisees—a Jewish religious group known for strictly observing the Old Covenant laws and customs—interrogated John. They also had been sent with the delegation and ²⁵asked John, "If you are not the Messiah, nor Elijah, nor the Great Prophet, then why are you out here baptizing? We Jewish people are used to ritual cleansing with water to cleanse us from our impurities before God. We are also used to a baptism that is reserved for Gentile converts to Judaism, one where they are totally cleansed to begin a new life. But we hear you are doing something different. So, what is this new way of baptizing people that you are doing and by whose authority are you doing it?

²⁶John replied, "I only baptize with water as a symbolic act of preparing people for the arrival of the One who is coming. However, there is One living among you whose authority you do not know about or recognize yet. He is the newness of life that is to come. ²⁷His work, even though it will come after mine, is vastly superior to anything I (or anyone else) can do! To give you an idea of how superior He

will be, let me say it this way: In His presence, I am not even worthy enough to be a slave who unties the straps of His sandals."

²⁸This interrogation by these Jewish religious leaders took place in Bethany—an area east of the Jordan River and not far from Jerusalem—because that is where John the Baptist was baptizing people.

> *2.1.2 The newness of life is here; the Spirit remains on Jesus (1:29–34).*

²⁹The next day, John the Baptist saw Jesus coming toward him and said: "Look and pay attention to what you see! Here He is, the Lamb of God—the One whose sacrifice will carry away our sinful, fallen condition that prohibits us from being in God's presence and makes us impure before Him. The Lamb of God's presence has a universal impact because He will take away the sins of the world! ³⁰He is the One I was talking about when I said, 'One is coming after me who is far greater than I am, because He is God in the flesh and existed before I was born.'

³¹"I had no special insight into which exact person the Messiah, who is the Christ, would be. I only knew what my place and purpose were. My place was to prepare the people of Israel, the ones whom God had been working through up to this point in history, for His arrival. My purpose was to ensure they were ready for when He arrived. That is why I have been baptizing with water so that the people of Israel might be prepared for the new way of life that Christ will give you."

³²Then John gave further evidence to solidify his personal witness to the truth about Jesus when he said: "In the past, we have known that God's Spirit was given to people sporadically, for a brief period of time. But I saw the Holy Spirit descend upon Him like a dove flying down from heaven and rest and remain on Him permanently!

³³"Again, I had no special insight into which exact person He would be. But when God sent me to baptize with water, He did tell me how I could recognize the Christ. God told me, 'You will see the Holy Spirit come down and permanently remain on a particular person. He is

the One who will baptize people with more than a physical, symbolic water baptism. He will baptize people with the Holy Spirit.' ³⁴I have seen everything God told me to look for, and it all happened to Jesus. As clearly and as certainly as I can tell you, Jesus is the Son of God, the Chosen One who brings delight to the heart of God the Father."

2.2 Decide to follow and learn from Jesus and discover a new kind of life (1:35–51).

2.2.1 Decide to follow Jesus because of who He is (1:35–42).

³⁵On the next day (the third day since Jesus began His ministry), John was standing with two of his disciples. ³⁶When John saw Jesus walking by, he said, "Look, here He is—the Lamb of God—the One whose sacrifice will carry away our sinful, fallen condition that makes us impure before God and prohibits us from entering into His presence!"

³⁷When these disciples heard John's testimony about Jesus, they decided to travel along with Jesus to learn more about Him. ³⁸When Jesus turned around, He saw them following. He asked them, "What is it you are looking for?"

They replied, "Rabbi (which is a respectful term meaning 'Teacher'), we would like to learn more from you and are wondering where you are staying?"

³⁹Jesus said, "Come with Me, and you will see." It was about four in the afternoon when they followed Jesus. They saw where He was staying and remained with Him, learning more about Him, the remainder of the day.

⁴⁰Andrew, the brother of Simon Peter was one of the first two who had followed Jesus. Andrew had also heard John the Baptist identify who Jesus was when He walked by. ⁴¹After realizing more of who Jesus is, the first thing Andrew did was find his brother, Simon. Andrew told Simon, "We have found the Messiah, who is the Christ—the

anointed One filled with God's power and Spirit who will decisively deliver God's people."

⁴²Then Andrew brought Simon to meet Jesus. When Jesus looked at him, He said, "You are Simon, son of John. But from now on you will have a new name. You will be called Cephas" (which is the Hebrew name for Peter that means "a Rock").

> 2.2.2 Decide to follow Jesus and discover what God will do (1:43–51).

⁴³The next day (on the fourth day since Jesus began His ministry), Jesus decided to go to Galilee, a region about fifty miles north of Jerusalem. When He arrived, Jesus found Philip and said to him, "Come and follow Me."

⁴⁴Phillip was from Bethsaida, a town just north of the Sea of Galilee. It was also Andrew's and Peter's home town. ⁴⁵Philip went and found his brother Nathanael and told him, "We have found the One whom Moses wrote about in the Law section of the Scriptures [the Old Testament]. He is the One the prophets wrote about in the Scriptures. His name is Jesus, the son of Joseph. He is from Nazareth."

⁴⁶Upon hearing this, Nathanael scoffed, "Nazareth, that little town a few miles southwest of the Sea of Galilee? Can anything good come out of that small town?"

Philip replied, "You should come and see for yourself."

⁴⁷When Jesus saw Nathanael coming toward Him, He said to Nathanael, "Here is a genuine Israelite—one who perfectly models what God intended the people of Israel to be. He is one in whom there is no deceit but only complete integrity."

⁴⁸Nathanael asked Him, "What makes You say that? You do not know me."

Jesus replied, "Before Philip came to you and told you about Me, when you thought you were all alone and no one knew where you were, I saw you sitting under that fig tree."

[49] Nathanael exclaimed, "Teacher, there is no way You could have known that unless you were God. I see who You are now. You are the Son of God, the King of Israel who will deliver God's people."

[50] Jesus said, "You believe just because I told you that I saw you when you were sitting under the fig tree, and you realized that I see and know all things. Well, let Me tell you, in the days ahead, you all are going to see and know things that are much greater than that!"

[51] Then Jesus continued, "Do you recall Jacob's Ladder in Genesis 28? In Jacob's dream, he saw the stairway to heaven. He saw God's angels ascending and descending on it. Jacob was amazed by what he briefly saw—a direct connection between heaven and earth. Well, you are going to see God connect heaven and earth permanently through the Son of Man."

3. Jesus and the Jewish Institutions: Realize that Jesus reveals and establishes a new way to be right with God (2:1–4:54).

> 3.1 Unlike Jewish rituals, Jesus reveals He has the resources to meet people's needs, transform one's relationship with God, and infuse people with new life (2:1–12). [The first sign revealing a deeper truth about God: Turning water into wine]
>
>> 3.1.1 A crisis develops around the lack of resources at a wedding, and Jesus is driven by God's mission for His life (2:1–4).

CHAPTER 2

¹Three days later (on the seventh day since Jesus began His ministry, similar to the seven days of creation), there was a wedding taking place at Cana in Galilee. In the Jewish culture of the Old Covenant, weddings were not only culturally important but also highly symbolic events. The wedding banquet was viewed as a model for what life will be like in heaven with God's victorious Messiah who is the Christ. Jesus' mother was at this wedding in Cana. ²Jesus and His disciples had also been invited and were attending this wedding celebration.

³While at this wedding, the supply of wine had run out. In the Jewish society of the Old Covenant, this was not only an embarrassing situation but also a crisis which would cause dishonor to the host. Jesus' mother saw the problem and told Him, "They have run out of wine; they will be completely dishonored. Can You do something about this dilemma?"

⁴Jesus replied, "While I understand the dilemma, getting involved in this human matter might distract Me from God's bigger purpose for My life. So, in this situation, I must think of you like you are any other woman asking Me to do something, and not as my mother asking for a family favor. God's mission for My life must be My focus, and My hour to act on behalf of the entire world has not yet come."

3.1.2 The stone jars used in ritual cleansing lack the resources to meet people's needs (2:5-6).

⁵Respecting what He said, she told the servants, "If He tells you to do something, do whatever He says."

⁶Standing nearby were six stone jars. The Old Covenant Jewish law required hands to be ceremonially washed before each meal. They used stone jars for the cleansing ritual because stone was seen as a pure material. These large, stone jars could hold between twenty to thirty gallons of water. However, these stone jars at the wedding—just like the Old Covenant Jewish ritual—were empty. They were missing out on their intended purpose (just like the people of Old Covenant Israel).

3.1.3 Jesus has the resources to meet people's needs and transforms the water into wine (2:7-8).

⁷But Jesus was about to do something new. He said to the servants, "Fill these jars with water." They filled them all to the brim.

⁸Then He said, "Now draw some of it out and take it to the wedding party's master of ceremonies to taste." They did as directed.

3.1.4 Jesus transforms the situation and infuses it with new life (2:9-10).

⁹When the master of ceremonies tasted the water that had been turned into wine, he had no idea where it came from (though the servants knew). The master of ceremonies then the called the bridegroom over and said, ¹⁰"Typically, everyone serves the best wine first. Then, after the guests have had plenty to drink and are less discriminating, they bring out the cheaper wine. But you have done something untypical and quite phenomenal. You have saved the best wine until now."

3.1.5 Jesus can transform one's relationship with God and infuse people with new life (2:11–12).

¹¹This act in Cana of Galilee was the first sign that Jesus did. These signs by Jesus are like miracles, but they go deeper by revealing something about God that had been hidden or unseen. This first sign revealed that while the Old Covenant Jewish rituals lack the resources to meet people's true needs, Jesus does not. Jesus demonstrated that He has the resources and ability to transform not only what has been created but also people's relationship with God. Unlike lifeless rituals, this first sign gave His followers a glimpse of God's glory. It demonstrated that Jesus is not merely a man, but He also radiates God's presence in the world and shows everyone God's infinite value and worth. When those following Jesus saw this sign, they believed in Him.

¹²After this, Jesus went down to Capernaum with His mother, brothers, and disciples. They stayed there for a few days.

3.2 Unlike the Jewish temple, Jesus reveals that the center of God's plan revolves around His own person, mission, and work (2:13–25).

3.2.1 The purpose of God's temple in the Old Covenant had been defiled (2:13–14).

¹³Each year, the Jewish people of the Old Covenant made a pilgrimage back to the temple in Jerusalem to celebrate the Passover Festival. This annual Passover Festival celebrated how God rescued the Old Covenant Israelites when He passed over their firstborn and freed them from Egyptian captivity. During the actual event of the Passover, God passed over homes that had been marked by the blood of a sacrificed lamb. During the Passover Festival, the people of Israel honored and remembered the Passover by participating in a symbolic meal that recalls the events of that night and by reflecting on how God delivered them from their bondage in Egypt. As part of the Passover Festival, the attendees made their sacrifices at the Temple, because it was considered the place where God lives—His home on earth.

When it was almost time for the annual Jewish Passover Festival, Jesus went up to Jerusalem.

¹⁴When Jesus arrived at the temple, He encountered an economy that was dishonoring to God's purpose for it. He found people in the temple's outer courtyard selling animals to be used in Passover sacrifices—cattle, sheep, and doves—at inflated prices. When Jesus arrived, He also found these money exchangers sitting at their tables spread out all across the temple court. They were there because the Jewish people who made the pilgrimage were required to pay a temple tax. Every Jewish person was expected to exchange their Roman or foreign currency for shekels, because shekels were considered a purer and higher quality currency. Thus, it was the only currency deemed acceptable at the temple, which they considered God's home on earth. However, the money exchangers were taking advantage of the Jewish pilgrims; they were trading the currency at inflated exchange rates.

3.2.2 Jesus calls everyone to refocus on the temple's true purpose (2:15–17).

¹⁵Frustrated at how the temple's purpose had been defiled and how the Passover Festival had been turned into a dishonoring economy, Jesus decided to disrupt it. He made a whip out of leather strips and chased all the animals out the temple court. He drove out both the cattle and sheep. He also overturned all the tables of the money exchangers, which scattered their coins everywhere. ¹⁶Then Jesus told the dove sellers, "Get these things out of here. Stop turning My Father's house into a house of money—a greedy marketplace! That is not why it is here, and it distracts everyone from the temple's true purpose."

¹⁷When this happened, Jesus' disciples remembered what the Scripture says in Psalm 69:9, "An abundance of passion toward Your dwelling place will consume me."

3.2.3 The authority of Jesus is questioned, and He foreshadows the sign of a greater temple—His crucified and resurrected body (2:18–20).

[18] Considering that Jesus had just driven out all the animals for sacrifice and all the money exchangers from the temple court (all of which had been allowed by Jewish leadership), the Jewish leaders of the Old Covenant questioned Jesus' authority to do what He had done. They asked, "What divine miracle or divine credential can You show us that will prove You have the personal authority to do these things?"

[19] Jesus answered, "You want a sign to prove My credentials? I will give you one. Destroy this temple, and in three days, I will raise it up again."

[20] The Jewish leaders replied, "Are You crazy? It has taken forty-six years to rebuild this much of the temple, and it will likely take us another thirty or forty years to finish it! And You think that if the temple is destroyed, You can rebuild it in three days?"

3.2.4 They fail to understand the greater Temple—Jesus' body (2:20–22).

[21] But they failed to understand what Temple Jesus was talking about. He was not talking about the stone temple that symbolically represented God's presence on earth. Instead, He was talking about a new Temple, the Temple that supersedes, surpasses, and replaces the old temple. Jesus was talking about His body as the Temple—the actual place where God's full presence in physical flesh and bone existed on earth.

[22] It was not until later, when Jesus was raised from the dead, that His disciples remembered what Jesus had said about His body being God's new Temple. When they understood what He said, they believed both the Scripture and the words that Jesus had spoken.

3.2.5 Jesus' teaching leads to a response (2:23–25).

²³While Jesus was in Jerusalem for the annual Passover Festival, many people saw the signs He did, these special acts done by Jesus that disclosed something formerly hidden about God. The result: Many people began to recognize His divine character and to trust in Him. ²⁴But Jesus did not entrust or commit Himself to them, because He already knew how untrustworthy they were. ²⁵Jesus did not need anyone to tell Him about human nature, because He knew everyone from the inside out; He knew what was in each person's heart.

3.3 Unlike Jewish rabbis, Jesus reveals a new way of belonging to God's kingdom and experiencing a new kind of life that eternally endures (3:1–21).

3.3.1 A new way of belonging to God requires a new birth (3:1–8).

CHAPTER 3

¹At the wedding at Cana, Jesus showed that the old wine of the Old Covenant Jewish ritual practices was incomplete. Instead, Jesus provides a new wine for the true needs of God's people, which replaces and surpasses the old perception of how God relates to the world. With the cleansing of the temple, Jesus indicated how the Jewish temple of the Old Covenant is an insufficient and incomplete dwelling place for God. Instead, Jesus said that His body is the true dwelling place of God on earth, which replaces and surpasses the old understanding of God's presence on earth. Now, we discover how Jesus replaces the old way of belonging to God with a new one.

Now there was a Pharisee named Nicodemus who was a member of the Sanhedrin. As a Pharisee, Nicodemus belonged to a Jewish religious group known for strictly observing the Old Covenant [Old Testament] laws and customs. As a member of the Sanhedrin, he was a part of the Jewish ruling council of seventy recognized leaders who were entrusted with leading the Old Covenant Jewish people. Nicodemus was familiar with Jesus' previous teachings and sought to have a conversation with Him.

²Maybe because he wanted secrecy, maybe because it was just the end of a busy day, or maybe because his old way of thinking represented spiritual darkness—Nicodemus came to talk with Jesus at night. He said, "Rabbi, even though You have not gone through any formal religious training, we recognize that You are a gifted teacher sent from God. No one could perform the miraculous things You are doing if God were not with him."

³Jesus replied, "We could talk about the nature of these signs and how I am able to do them, but there is something far more important we need to discuss. Let Me tell you this vital truth: No one can see the kingdom of God and experience His salvation unless they are born from above."

⁴Nicodemus responded, "How can anyone be born anew, a second time, when they have already grown up? Can human nature really be changed or start over? It is not possible. One cannot enter a second time into their mother's womb!"

⁵Jesus answered, "Naturally speaking, you are right, but do not assume your natural birth or innate goodness is enough to make you right with God. It is not. Something more is needed. This is important, so let Me share this vital truth with you again: No one can enter the kingdom of God unless they experience a spiritual cleansing and regeneration from the heavenly realm. The prophet Ezekiel, in Ezekiel 36:25–27, described this new, spiritual regeneration as being born of both water and the Spirit. ⁶And this new, spiritual regeneration has a simple logic to it. A person is born physically of human parents, for flesh gives birth to flesh. But a person is born spiritually by the Holy Spirit, for Spirit gives birth to spirit.

⁷Jesus continued, saying, "As a respected leader of the Jewish teachings, you should not be surprised when I tell you that, if you are to belong to God, this new spiritual birth is not optional. You must be

born from above, straight from God. ⁸This new birth is not something that human beings can control through a religious system or practice. It has a mysterious, uncontrollable, divine nature to it. For example, the wind blows wherever it pleases. You hear its sound, but you cannot tell where it comes from or where it is going. It is this same way with everyone born from above, born of the Spirit."

> *3.3.2 A new way of belonging to God requires believing in Jesus Christ (3:9–18).*

⁹Nicodemus said, "I am baffled by this teaching. How can this new birth be possible?"

¹⁰Jesus answered, "You are a respected religious leader and Jewish teacher, and yet you do not understand these basic things? ¹¹Let Me tell you this truth: We talk about what we have seen and know to be true. We speak from first-hand experience of these realities. Yet, instead of accepting the evidence I have given you, you refuse it and reject it. ¹²I have already told you plainly about how God can transform people through a new birth—about a spiritual regeneration that you can see right here on earth. If you do not believe Me about these things, how will you ever trust what I tell you about heavenly realities, the things that you cannot see right now? ¹³No one has ever gone into heaven except for the One that came from heaven—the Son of Man who came directly from the realm of God's presence and reveals Him to you.

¹⁴In the Old Covenant Scripture, in Numbers 21:4–9, when Moses lifted up the bronze snake on a pole in the wilderness, those who looked to it were delivered and healed. In a similar but eternally better way, the Son of Man must be lifted up ¹⁵so that everyone who trusts in Him will have a new kind of life with God."

¹⁶This is an entirely new way of belonging to God. God's love is no longer limited to a select, special few. Instead, God's love is universally available to a world that is in desperate need of it. Out of the unfathomable depths of God's love, He gave up His one and only Son so that everyone who trusts in Him will not experience eternal destruction

but receive a new, supernatural life—a new kind of life that will never end. ¹⁷God did not send His Son into the world to condemn it. The world is already spiritually dark enough on its own. It already stands condemned by its own darkness. Instead, God sent His Son into the world to provide a way to escape the spiritual darkness and the destruction it brings. God sent His Son into the world to reveal a path of salvation that is open to everyone through Him.

¹⁸However, whether one trusts in God's Son is the decisive factor in determining who belongs to God, for He is the One through whom God saves those who believe. Whoever trusts in the Son is not condemned. But whoever does not trust in His Son stands condemned already in their spiritual darkness, for they do not trust in God's path of salvation offered to all through the Son of God.

3.3.3 A new way of belonging to God brings His light into life (3:19–21).

¹⁹This is the ultimate human crisis and God's verdict on it: God sent His true light into the world, but people loved their spiritual darkness instead of God's light. They wanted to live for themselves and wallow in their own darkness instead of living to please God and living in His light. ²⁰Every person, whether they realize it or not, does evil because their affections and desires focus on themselves and the things of this world instead of God. Inside a cloud of illusion, denial, and deception, they actually hate God's illuminating light. They do not want to come into God's light because it will show all the evil things they do, and they do not want their evil deeds to be exposed. ²¹But whoever desires to live in the truth and to do what is right comes into the light. By coming into the light, they show that the things they do have been done by God, that He is the One who has been working in and through them.

3.4 Unlike Jewish perspectives on baptism, Jesus is the focus of God's work in the world; all focus should be on Him (3:22–36).

3.4.1 A question about baptism raises a bigger question: Where should the focus be in one's relationship with God? (3:22–26).

²²After this conversation with Nicodemus about a new way to belong to God, Jesus and His disciples left Jerusalem and went into the Judean countryside. While there, Jesus spent time with His disciples as they were baptizing those who responded to Jesus' teaching. ²³At the same time, John the Baptist was also baptizing in Aenon, which is a small town on the Jordan River not far from Salim and near the Samaritans. People were coming to John the Baptist for baptism there, for there was plenty of water at Aenon. ²⁴(This was before John the Baptist was put in prison.)

²⁵During this time, an argument broke out between some of John the Baptist's followers and a Jewish person about purification before God and the nature of baptism. They debated whether the baptisms they were performing were just a ceremonial ritual cleansing (the Jewish person's argument) or were necessary to initiate a new relationship with God (John the Baptist's followers' argument). ²⁶As part of the discussion, Jesus' ministry and the baptizing that His followers were doing came up. So, they came to John the Baptist with a question about it and said, "Teacher, remember that man who was with you on the other side of Jordan, the one you testified about? He is also baptizing people, and it seems that more people are going to Him instead of us! Since our baptism is a symbol of a new relationship with God, should not more people be coming to us to be baptized?"

3.4.2 Jesus Christ is the focus of God's work in the world (3:27–30).

²⁷John replied, "A person must be content with what they have received from God in heaven. ²⁸I am more than content with the role God has given me. You yourselves should know that because you were there when I gave public testimony that declared, 'I am not the Messiah who is the Christ, the anointed One filled with God's power

and Spirit who will decisively deliver God's people. But I have been sent ahead of the Christ to prepare the way for His arrival.'

²⁹"The purpose of my role is like being the friend of the Bridegroom at a wedding. The Bridegroom is the one who marries the bride. The friend of the Bridegroom is not the focus. Instead, the friend is full of joy and happy to stand beside the Bridegroom during the occasion, happy to hear His voice and celebrate what He is doing. And now that the wedding is over, and the marriage is off to a good start, I am overflowing with joy and more than content with my role in celebrating the occasion.

3.4.3 Jesus Christ should be the focus of one's life with God (3:31–36).

³⁰"As for Jesus, if His followers are baptizing more than us, then that is great! Why? Because Jesus is the One that all focus should be on. My role—and any baptism associated with me—is and always will be below His. Allegiance to Him is eternally more important than allegiance to me. His importance in your hearts, minds, and lives must infinitely increase; mine must decrease.

³¹"Jesus is superior and must become greater for a wide variety of reasons. He is the One who comes from above—whose origins come directly from God in heaven. He is greater than any human being who ever has or ever will exist. Human beings are born naturally, have human limitations, and speak like human beings. The One who comes directly from God in heaven is born supernaturally, is not limited in any way, and speaks divine thoughts. The One who comes directly from God is infinitely greater and superior to anyone else, ever.

³²"Jesus speaks from personal experience with God the Father. He testifies to the evidence that He has seen and heard first-hand. Yet people refuse to believe what He tells them. ³³Whoever has accepted Jesus has made a firm decision about God's truth. They have authenticated and confirmed God's truth by staking their entire life on following Jesus and His way.

³⁴"Jesus is the One sent from God. He speaks the words of God, for He is the only One the Spirit fully remains on and constantly fills without limit. ³⁵Jesus has the complete love and trust of God the Father. God the Father has entrusted everything into His Son's hands and given Him authority over all.

³⁶"As a result of Jesus being the One sent from heaven who speaks the truth to us, everyone faces a simple choice. Whoever trusts in Jesus, God's Son, has a new kind of life that eternally endures. But whoever disobeys God and does not trust in His Son will not experience this newness of life with God that eternally endures. Instead, God's wrath will remain on them."

> 3.5 Unlike Jewish debates on where and how to worship God, Jesus reveals a new way to worship God; offers a new, eternal provision of a life in direct connection with God; and breaks down barriers between people (4:1–42).
>
> *3.5.1 Jesus provides a new way to worship God (4:1–26).*

CHAPTER 4

¹Now the Pharisees—members of a Jewish group dedicated to strictly observing the Old Covenant laws and customs—heard that Jesus was baptizing more disciples than John the Baptist. ²(Although, they had heard wrong. It was actually His disciples, because Jesus did not baptize anyone.) ³When Jesus knew that the Pharisees had heard about the new way of belonging to God He was proclaiming, He left Judea (in southern Israel) and set out for Galilee (in northern Israel).

⁴To get there by the shortest and easiest route, Jesus had to go through Samaria. The Jewish people of the Old Covenant typically looked down on the Samaritan race because of what happened in their religious history. Nearly 800 years earlier [in the 8th Century B.C.], when the Assyrians conquered the ten northern tribes of Israel, they

intermingled their race with the Jewish race. Because of this racial intermingling, the Pharisees and the remaining tribes of Israel considered the Samaritans to be an impure race that God no longer worked through. As a result, they avoided associating with Samaritans.

⁵While Jesus and His disciples were traveling through Samaria, they came to a Samaritan town called Sychar. Sychar is near the plot of ground Jacob gave to his son Joseph in the Old Covenant book of Genesis. ⁶It was an important spot in early Jewish history, and Jacob constructed a well there. Jesus, tired from the long walk, sat down at Jacob's well. It was around noon, the hottest part of the day.

⁷Even though women typically only came to the well in the morning or the early evening, a Samaritan woman came to the well at noon to draw water. She came to the well during this time of day because she was considered a social outcast in the community. Also, since this woman was a Samaritan, it would be unusual for a devout Jewish person—following the Jewish customs of the day—to talk to her. Even more, it would be very uncommon for a religious leader who was by Himself to converse with any woman, let alone a woman considered a social outcast. Yet Jesus broke with the Jewish customs and asked the woman, "Would you mind giving Me a drink of water?" ⁸(He was alone at this time because the disciples had gone into town to buy food.)

⁹The woman was taken aback with surprise that He was talking to her. She replied, "You are a Jew, and I am both a Samaritan and a woman. Jewish people normally never talk to Samaritans. So, why are You asking me for a drink?"

¹⁰Jesus responded, "If you only knew how universally open God's love is and who I am, you would be asking Me for a drink. And I would give you a living water that would move and flow within you, giving you life in every sense of the word."

¹¹"Sir," the woman said, "You do not have anything to draw water with, and this well is deep. Besides, we are in a very dry area, and there is no moving or living water here that I am aware of. So, how are You

going to get or offer me living water when no one else has found any? ¹²This well here was dug by our ancestor Jacob. He, his sons, and his livestock all drank from this well's water. It is our main water source. You do not claim to be a better provider of water and a greater person than Jacob, do You?"

¹³Jesus replied, "Everyone who drinks of this water—from this old, sacred well—will be thirsty again and again. Their deeper thirst will never be satisfied. ¹⁴But whoever drinks the water that I give, water from a new well, will never thirst again. The water I give provides one with an endless spring of water that flows with a new kind of life that eternally satisfies and endures."

¹⁵The woman said, "That sounds amazing! Please give me this water so that I will never be thirsty again. I will be glad not to have to come to this well anymore."

¹⁶Jesus saw the woman was not comprehending the deeper, spiritual meaning. He said, "I am afraid you are still limiting yourself to a physical and natural understanding. So, I tell you what, go get your husband and bring him back here with you."

¹⁷The woman replied, "I do not have a husband."

Jesus said, "That is exactly right. You do not have a husband. ¹⁸Instead, you have had five husbands, and the man that you live with now is not your husband either. So, yes, you told Me the truth when you said you do not have a husband."

¹⁹"How did You know that!" she said. "You must be a prophet! ²⁰As a prophet, maybe you can answer one of the biggest debates we Samaritans have with the Jewish people. My Samaritan ancestors worshiped here at Mount Gerizim because it was the first altar that Abraham ever built to God; it was viewed as a source of life via Jacob's well; and it was the place where Joshua entered into the promised land after the exodus. But you Jewish people say that Jerusalem is the place where we should worship God because David selected it; he

brought the tabernacle there, and Solomon built God's temple there. So, which one of these locations is the right place to worship God?"

²¹Jesus replied, "Dear woman, believe what I am about to tell you. The debate about which location in the Old Covenant Scriptures is the correct place for worshipping God—either at Mount Gerizim or in Jerusalem—is of little importance anymore. A new way of worshipping God is coming; the hour of its arrival will change how you worship. ²²Also, I am afraid your Samaritan views are not in line with God's trajectory and plan for salvation. We Jewish people worship in line with God's path and plan, for He said the Messiah who brings salvation would come through the Jewish people.

²³"But the time is coming—and is now here among us—when the true worshippers will worship the Father in Spirit and in truth. Those who worship in Spirit and in truth are the kind of worshippers the Father seeks. ²⁴Why? Because God is Spirit and has a dynamic, life-giving character. So, those who worship Him must worship Him with a life that is dynamically animated by God's Spirit and informed by His revealed truth."

²⁵The woman replied, "Thankfully, we will find out how to rightly worship God one day. In Deuteronomy 18:18, it teaches that a great prophet, a Messiah, will come after Moses and decisively and eternally deliver God's people. I know the Messiah, the one they call the Christ, is coming. When the Christ arrives, He will explain everything to us."

²⁶Using the same "I am" language that God uses to identify Himself in the Old Covenant, Jesus said to her, "I am the Messiah who is the Christ!"

3.5.2 Jesus offers a new life of eternal provision from God (4:27-38).

²⁷At this point, Jesus' disciples returned. Because of the cultural norms, they were shocked to see Jesus talking to the woman. But they were even more shocked that He was talking to a Samaritan woman (since the Jewish people looked down on their cultural and religious background). However, even though the disciples were surprised at

this conversation, none of them had enough personal courage to ask Jesus, "What was so important that made You talk to this Samaritan woman?" or "Why on earth are You talking to her?"

²⁸Yet, the woman had personal courage. After learning more about Jesus from their conversation, she ran back to her town. She had so much zeal that, in her excitement, she left her water jar behind. When she arrived back at town, she told them, ²⁹"Come and see a man who knew everything about me and everything I ever did! Could this man be the Messiah—the anointed one from God who will deliver God's people? Come and find out!" ³⁰Upon hearing this, the people left the town and went out to see Jesus.

³¹While the woman was out telling others in her town about Jesus, the disciples were having a conversation with Him. They had been sent out to get food and had brought it back. Yet, He was not eating any of it. The disciples urged Him, "Teacher, You really should eat something."

³²But Jesus replied, "I have food to eat that you know nothing about."

³³The disciples were puzzled. They asked each other, "Where did He get food? Did someone else bring Him some while we were gone?"

³⁴Then Jesus elevated the conversation beyond physical food by explaining to them, "The food that nourishes Me and keeps Me going is to do the will of One who sent Me and to finish the work He gave Me to do. ³⁵Do you know the local proverb that says, 'Four months more and then the harvest?' That proverb highlights the joyful expectation of the harvest that the planter anticipates. He is excited to plant, knowing that in due time the harvest will come. Well, I am telling you to wake up, open your eyes, and look around. Right now, the fields are already ripe for the harvest. You do not have to wait for it at all. The time for harvest is right now!

³⁶"Right now, the one who reaps the harvest is already being paid. He does not have to rely on an old approach of waiting on an agricultural cycle to gather the crops. Instead, right now, the reaper can gather

the fruit of God's spiritual harvest—the people who are brought into God's life eternal. Right now, in God's new spiritual work, both the one who sows the seed and the reaper who harvests it can be glad at the same time.

³⁷"You know that saying, 'One sows and another reaps.' Well, in this case, that saying is true. ³⁸I sent you to reap a crop that you have not labored to produce. Others have already done the hard work for you; they have prepared the way for this religious harvest. Yet, you are members of the same team. Now, you get to step in to reap the results of their labor. As members of the same team, you both can be glad at the gathering of this eternal harvest."

> *3.5.3 Jesus breaks down barriers between people as they come to believe in Him (4:39–42).*

³⁹The harvest was indeed happening right around them. Many Samaritans from the town believed in Jesus because of the woman's eyewitness account. She was personally sharing what she had learned, saying, "This man knew everything about me and knew everything I ever did." ⁴⁰When the Samaritans came to Jesus, they begged Him to stay with them. So, Jesus stayed there with them for two days. ⁴¹During this time, many more believed because of His message.

⁴²They said to the woman, "We no longer believe just because of what you told us. Now, we believe because we have heard Jesus for ourselves. We now know for ourselves that this man truly is the Savior of the world."

3.6 Unlike the Jewish response, Jesus reveals that believing in Him is not about His miracles but about trusting in who He is—the Son of God (4:43-54).

3.6.1 Many people only look to God because of what they think He can do for them (4:43-45).

⁴³After spending two days in Samaria (where Jesus was appreciated more for who He was), Jesus left for Galilee (where He was appreciated more for the miracles He performed). ⁴⁴Jesus Himself had anticipated this reaction in Israel when He said, "A prophet who speaks a timely message of God's truth is not honored in His own country." ⁴⁵So, when Jesus arrived back in Israel at Galilee, they welcomed Him. However, the people of Israel only welcomed Him because they had seen all the things that He did in Jerusalem during the Passover Festival. They were anticipating only the things Jesus might be able to do for them, as opposed to being excited about who He was or the mission He was sent to accomplish.

3.6.2 More than a miracle worker who meets needs, Jesus is the Son of God (4:46-54). [The second sign revealing a deeper truth about God: Healing the royal official's son]

⁴⁶As He was traveling through Galilee, Jesus came back to Cana, the place where He had turned water into wine. While Jesus was in the area, in the nearby town of Capernaum, there was a government official in King Herod Antipas' court whose son was deathly sick. ⁴⁷When the royal official heard that Jesus had come back from Judea to Galilee, he went up the hills to Cana. He asked Jesus to come down from Cana to the shore of Capernaum, which was about twenty miles away, to heal his son, who was so ill that he could die at almost any moment.

⁴⁸Jesus said to him, "Unless you people see miraculous signs and wonders, you all will never believe."

⁴⁹The royal official appealed to Jesus very directly, "Sir, come with me before my child dies."

⁵⁰Jesus replied just as directly, "Go; your son will live." The man took Jesus at His word and left.

⁵¹As the royal official was traveling on the way back home, his servants came and met him on the way. They told him the news that his son was recovering and going to live. ⁵²He asked them what hour his son began to get better. They said to him, "It was yesterday, at one o'clock in the afternoon that the fever suddenly left him." ⁵³The father knew that one o'clock was the exact hour Jesus had said to him, "Your son will live." In response, the royal official and his entire household believed in Jesus for who He was, and not just for miracles He could do.

⁵⁴This was now the second sign that Jesus did after coming from Judea to Galilee. The second sign pointed to a deeper truth about God, revealing that Jesus has the power to heal, even from a distance.

4. Jesus and Jewish festivals: Realize that Jesus defines a new way of life dedicated to God (5:1–10:42).

4.1 Jesus and the Festival of Sabbath: Jesus is the Son of God who has His power and authority over life and His ability to give life to others (5:1–47).

4.1.1 The alleged criminal activity: Jesus breaks the religious and cultural norm by healing and giving the gift of life on the Sabbath (5:1–15). [The third sign revealing a deeper truth about God: Healing the paralyzed man]

CHAPTER 5

THE ACT: CHRIST HEALS THE PARALYTIC MAN (5:1–9)

¹Three times per year, the custom was for all Jewish people to travel to Jerusalem to celebrate certain religious festivals. These religious festivals were dedicated times when the Jewish people gave special thanks

to God for what He had done for His people, and they celebrated His good gifts to them. They were also key markers of devotion in a cycle of life dedicated to and focused on God.

As the time for one of these religious festivals approached, Jesus returned to Jerusalem to celebrate it. ²Inside the city of Jerusalem, near the Sheep Gate (where there was also a sheep market), there was a large pool with five porches. In Aramaic, it was called the pool of Bethesda, which means the "place of mercy." It was called Bethesda (or place of mercy) because it was believed that, at appointed seasons, its flowing waters could cure the diseases of whomever stepped into the water first. ³As a result, large crowds of sick and disabled people—the blind, lame, or paralyzed—lay on the porches beside the pool. They lay there waiting for the right moment hoping to be the first to jump into the water. [Some manuscripts include: "⁴During these appointed seasons, it was believed that an angel of the Lord would come down and stir up the waters, giving them healing power. The first person into the pool after each disturbance would be cured of any disease."]

⁵One man who was there had been a disabled invalid for thirty-eight years. ⁶When Jesus saw the invalid man lying there and learned that he had been in this disabled condition for a long time, He asked the man, "Do you want to get well?"

⁷The disabled man said, "Sir, I would love to, but when the waters are stirred and supposedly capable of providing healing power, I have no one who can put me into the pool first. While I am trying my best to be the first one into the pool, someone else always gets in before I can."

⁸Jesus responded, "Let Me change all of that for you. Right now, I want you to stand up, pick up your mat, and start walking."

⁹Immediately, the man was healed. He stood up, picked up his mat, and started walking. But this man's healing happened on the Sabbath.

THE OCCASION: CHRIST HEALS THE PARALYTIC MAN ON THE SABBATH (5:10-15).

¹⁰The Sabbath was supposed to be a day of rest fully dedicated to God. No one was supposed to work on the Sabbath. The Jewish religious leaders—in the tradition they had created around the Old Covenant Scriptures—defined what could and could not be done on the Sabbath. This man carrying his mat on the Sabbath was prohibited by their tradition. In their tradition, it was viewed as a serious infraction dishonoring God. The penalty for breaking the Sabbath was being stoned to death.

So, these Jewish leaders said to the man who had been healed, "What do you think you are doing? Today is the Sabbath! It is against God's law for you to carry your mat!"

¹¹But the healed man responded, "The man who healed me told me to 'pick up my mat and start walking.' Since He had enough power and authority to heal me, I thought it was appropriate and important to do what He said."

¹²Since the Pharisees equated their traditions with God's will, they demanded, "What type of person would commit such a serious breach of God's law! Who is the man who told you to pick up your mat and start walking?"

¹³But the man did not know who had healed him, because there were many people in that place at that time. And, after healing the man, Jesus had slipped away into the crowd.

¹⁴A little bit later, Jesus found the healed man in the temple area. Jesus instructed him, "Look at you! You have become well again! This healing will last, but only if you stop the sinful behavior—those actions that are displeasing to God. If you do not stop them, then something worse than being an invalid is going to happen to you."

¹⁵Having discovered Jesus' identity, the man then went and told the Jewish leaders that Jesus was the One who had healed him.

4.1.2 The Deliberation: Even though some people may be unsure, Jesus, as the Son of God, has the authority to give life any time He wants (5:16–30).

THE REALITY: NOT EVERYONE WILL ACCEPT THAT JESUS IS THE SON OF GOD (5:16-18).

¹⁶So why were these Jewish leaders out to get Jesus and bring Him to trial? The first reason they began to prosecute Jesus was that Jesus was in the habit of doing things on the Sabbath. In their legalistic tradition, they had developed a long list of customs for what people could and could not do on the Sabbath. For anyone who broke their Sabbath customs, they thought they were obligated to punish them. And they thought they were doing the right thing before God by administering punishment for such religious lawlessness.

¹⁷Even though the Pharisees prohibited people from working on the Sabbath, Jesus knew they still believed God did certain types of work on the Sabbath. So, while responding to their accusation, Jesus saw an opportunity to clarify who He was. He said, "My Father is always at work. Every day, He is sustaining the universe and overseeing life and death. Even on the Sabbath, He continues working while calling others to enjoy a day of rest and devotion. My Father exercises His divine prerogative on the Sabbath as He sees fit. I am His Son, and I too am working as I see fit."

¹⁸The second reason they began to prosecute Jesus and bring Him to trial was this: By claiming to be God, they believed Jesus had committed blasphemy. Blasphemy was a horrible offense punishable by death. For this reason, these Jewish leaders sought to prosecute Jesus for a capital offense. They wanted to see Him killed. From their perspective, not only was Jesus breaking the Sabbath law and tradition, but He was also claiming that God was his Father, making Himself equal with God.

THE DEFENSE: REGARDLESS OF WHETHER PEOPLE ACCEPT HIM, JESUS IS THE SON OF GOD, AND ALL SHOULD BELIEVE IN HIM (5:19-23).

¹⁹Jesus explained to them, "Since you are putting Me on a pseudo-trial here and have leveled two charges against Me——breaking the Sabbath

and blasphemy against God—let Me tell you this truth: The Son of God can do nothing by Himself. The divine connection between the Father and the Son is perfect. The Son never acts independently of the Father's will. He obeys, follows, and learns everything directly from the Father. As a result, the Son has only learned to do what He has seen the Father do. And since the divine connection between them is a perfect union, whatever the Father does, the Son also does.

20"How is such a claim possible? What is My rationale to support it? I will give you three reasons. My first reason: The Father loves the Son with an ongoing, constant affection. The Father shows Him everything He is doing and includes the Son in all things. What you saw earlier—the healing of the disabled man—is just a small taste of the greater works the Father will show Him. Later, when you see those things the Son will do, you are going to be amazed!

21"My second reason: The Father gives the Son power and authority over life. Just as the Father raises the dead and gives them new life, so the Son also gives life to anyone He wants to.

22"My third reason: The Father gives the Son His power and authority to judge over all things. In fact, the Father does not judge anyone. He has entrusted all judgment to the Son. 23You see, the Son is the Father's very presence and representation in the world. He gives the Son the power to judge so that everyone will honor the Son just as much as they honor the Father. But the opposite is also true: Anyone who fails to honor the Son does not honor God the Father who sent Him, and they will face His judgment.

MAKE A DECISION: THOSE WHO TRUST IN JESUS WILL HAVE A NEW KIND OF LIFE THAT ETERNALLY ENDURES; THOSE WHO DO NOT BELIEVE IN JESUS WILL BE GUILTY OF THEIR UNBELIEF AND CONDEMNED (5:24-30).

24"And do you realize that the Son's life-giving power and authority to judge are already active in the world right now? Let Me tell you this truth: Whoever hears My word—accepting who I am and believing My message—and trusts in the Father who sent Me has a new kind of life, the kind of life that will endure eternally. Those who trust in Me will not be judged. Having the new kind of life that eternally endures living within them, they have crossed over from death to life.

[25] "I have told you a little about this new kind of life, but I cannot stress enough how vitally important the reality of this truth is! The time is coming—indeed, the time has now come—when those who are spiritually dead will hear the voice of the Son of God. Those who listen and respond to His voice will live in a new kind of life, one that eternally endures.

[26] "And to make this point about His power clear, the Father has given the Son authority over two distinct things. First, just as the Father is the source of life, He has granted the Son His same life-giving power. [27] Second, because He is the Son of Man—the One who embodies the true character of humanity in perfect relationship to God (as it was meant to be)—the Father has given the Son divine authority to exercise judgment over all humankind.

[28] "Do not be surprised or shocked by what I am saying. Indeed, a future hour is coming when all who are dead and buried will hear the Son's voice calling to them. [29] They all will experience a general resurrection from the dead and face His judgment. For those who have done good works motivated by their faith, they will rise and live this new kind of life—a life that is lived in relationship with God and eternally endures. And for those who have done what is evil, they will rise to receive God's judgment and just condemnation for their own guilt before Him.

[30] "I do not make My judgments alone. I make all My judgments in perfect harmony with what I hear from the Father. My judgment is just, because I do not seek to carry out My own will but to carry out and please the will of the One who sent Me.

4.1.3 The Evidence for Jesus: All the evidence of God's work in the world shows that Jesus is the Son of God who will save the world (5:31–47).

WITNESS 1: GOD THE FATHER'S WORK IN THE WORLD SERVES AS EVIDENCE THAT JESUS IS THE SON OF GOD WHO SAVES THE WORLD (5:31-32).

³¹"I realize that in Jewish trials, the Old Covenant [Old Testament] teaches that one's own self-testimony is not enough; it is inadmissible evidence. In these trials, more than one witness is needed to confirm someone's testimony. I do not want to treat this pseudo-trial dialogue that we are engaged in any differently. I realize that, for you, My testimony about Myself is not valid enough. So, let Me share several witnesses with you who corroborate My claims.

³²"My first witness is God the Father. He has testified about Me throughout human history. He is the most reliable witness of all. I know His abundant evidence about Me is spread across the universe and declares the truth about Me.

WITNESS 2: THE TEACHING OF JOHN THE BAPTIST—WHO WAS SENT TO PREPARE PEOPLE TO RECEIVE THE CHRIST—SERVES AS EVIDENCE THAT JESUS IS THE SON OF GOD WHO SAVES THE WORLD (5:33-35).

³³"My second witness is John the Baptist. You sent investigators to inquire about Me to John the Baptist. Did he not give you a reliable witness and testimony about Me? He spoke the truth about Me to you. ³⁴It is not that I need the testimony of a human witness. However, I mention him so that you might hear his truthful testimony through a means you can relate to and understand so that you will be saved. ³⁵John the Baptist was a lamp burning and shining a very bright light. For a while, you were willing to enjoy the illumination of his message, but you have missed the One his light was pointing to, the One who is God's light.

WITNESS 3: ALL THE WORKS THAT JESUS HAS DONE WHILE ON EARTH SERVE AS EVIDENCE THAT JESUS IS THE SON OF GOD WHO SAVES THE WORLD (5:36).

³⁶"My third witness is My works, the things I have done. The works that I have done provide you with an even greater witness than the

testimony of John the Baptist. I am doing the work My Father gave Me to complete. My works—the very things I am doing—testify to you about who I am and prove that the Father has sent Me.

WITNESS 1 (REVISITED): GOD'S WORK THROUGHOUT HUMAN HISTORY SERVES AS EVIDENCE THAT JESUS IS THE SON OF GOD WHO SAVES THE WORLD (5:37-38).

37"And, as mentioned before, My first witness is the Father who sent Me. Throughout history, He has been testifying and giving proof about Me. But you have never heard His voice or seen Him in person. 38Yet it is clear that you do not listen to His message. It is clear that you are not keeping His teaching in your hearts because you do not believe the One He has sent.

WITNESS 4: THE OLD COVENANT SCRIPTURES SERVE AS EVIDENCE THAT JESUS IS THE SON OF GOD WHO SAVES THE WORLD (5:39-44).

39"My fourth witness is Scripture. You all search and study the Scriptures because you think those words will somehow, by themselves, give you eternal life. But do you not realize that those written words of Scripture have a common purpose: they are all intended to point you toward Me! 40Yet, here I am, right in front of you. But you refuse to come to Me and receive the type of life you are seeking and wanting—a new kind of life that eternally endures.

41"I tell you these things plainly because I do not need human praise or approval. 42I know what is in your hearts, and I know the love of God is not in them, that His love is not in you. God is not your focus nor your driving motivation. 43I have come to you humbly, in the full character of My Father's name, and you have not accepted Me. However, if someone else comes full of boasting, bragging, or boldly elevating their self-importance and worth, you will gladly receive them. 44No wonder you do not get it. You spend all your time focused on receiving honor, being praised, or being valued by one another. You do not make receiving honor, being praised, or being valued by God your number one priority.

WITNESS 5: THE LAW, TEACHING, AND WORK OF MOSES SERVE AS EVIDENCE THAT JESUS IS THE SON OF GOD WHO SAVES THE WORLD (5:45-47).

⁴⁵"But do not think I have come just to accuse you of serious errors before My Father. Instead of Me, My fifth witness, Moses, will be your accuser. He will be the one who says you are wrong according to God's law. Yes, that is right. Moses, the one whom you claim to put all your hopes in, will be the one who brings accusations of guilt against you before God. ⁴⁶Why would he accuse you? Because if you had believed in what Moses taught, you would have believed in Me. Everything Moses wrote was pointing to Me, and you missed it. ⁴⁷And if you do not believe what Moses has written about Me, then how in the world are you going to believe anything I have to say?"

4.2 Jesus and the Festival of Passover: Jesus is the Son of God who meets people's needs by providing for their ultimate salvation and by giving them the sustenance they need as they travel through life (6:1–71).

4.2.1 Christ feeds 5,000: Unlike the old way that did not fully meet peoples lasting needs, Jesus is the Christ who meets people's needs by providing ultimate deliverance and salvation to God's people (6:1–15). [The fourth sign revealing a deeper truth about God: Feeding the 5,000]

CHAPTER 6

¹Some time later, Jesus crossed over to the far side of the Sea of Galilee, which is also known as the Sea of Tiberias. ²Jesus and His disciples sought some rest and a retreat from the masses. However, many people had seen the miraculous healings Jesus had been doing among the sick. As a result, a large crowd of people followed Him wherever He went. ³When Jesus had crossed the sea, He went up on the eastern hillside and sat down surrounded by His disciples. ⁴It was almost time for the Jewish Passover Festival, and all the following events and conversations happened in the context of that festival and what it means.

⁵When Jesus looked up and saw a large crowd coming toward Him, He said to Phillip, "Where can we buy enough bread to feed all of these people?" ⁶Of course, Jesus already knew what He was about to do; He asked this question to test Phillip's focus and perspective.

⁷Phillip answered, "The crowd is huge! Just to buy enough bread to give each person a minimal amount, it would take over eight month's wages!"

⁸Then Andrew (who was Simon Peter's brother) spoke up, ⁹"There is a young boy here who has five barley loaves (which were each about the size of a pita bread) and two small fish. But what good is so little when the need is so big?"

¹⁰Then Jesus gave the disciples these directions: "Have all of these people sit down and relax." There was a good amount of grass there, so they all sat down—all 10,000 plus (5,000 men and at least 5,000 more women and children). ¹¹Jesus then took the loaves, gave thanks to God, and distributed them to those who were seated. He did the same things with the fish. Through His power and supernatural work, the food was multiplied in their presence, and it provided enough for everyone to eat as much as they wanted.

¹²When everyone had eaten all they desired, Jesus instructed the disciples, "Gather up all of the pieces and leftovers; let nothing be wasted." ¹³So they picked up the pieces left from those who had eaten. They filled up twelve baskets of leftovers. Just the baskets of leftovers alone (from the food that Jesus had provided) far exceeded the original amount of five barely loves.

¹⁴When the people saw this sign—this event that revealed something divine and pointed toward a greater work of God—they recognized its significant connection. They said, "For many years, we have celebrated the Passover. One of the miracles we remember during the Passover Festival was done by Moses. In the past, God worked through Moses to miraculously feed all the people of Israel with manna from heaven. However, we have longed for the day when Deuteronomy 18:15–19 would be fulfilled, where it says a prophet like Moses but greater than

he would arrive and ultimately provide for the deliverance of God's people. And now, we have seen Moses' miracle of manna surpassed. We have just seen the treasures of heaven opened to supply us with food beyond what we can imagine. Surely this man is the prophet mentioned in Deuteronomy 18:15–19. Surely He is the Messiah who is the Christ, the One who is to come into the world!"

¹⁵Jesus realized they were only thinking about the Messiah as someone who would meet their needs and as a military, political figure who would overthrow Herod and the Romans. Jesus realized they would try to seize Him and declare Him to be this type of king. So, rather than allowing their misguided zeal to misrepresent His true purpose, He withdrew from them and retreated into the mountain hillside by Himself.

> *4.2.2 Christ walks on water: Unlike the old water miracle that temporarily provided water from a rock, Jesus has power and authority over water itself (6:16–24). [The fifth sign revealing a deeper truth about God: Walking on water]*

¹⁶Later that evening, Jesus' disciples went down to the seashore. ¹⁷It was now dark, and Jesus had not yet rejoined them. So, they got into a boat and set out to cross the sea and go to Capernaum. ¹⁸Since the sea lies in a deep valley and pulls in cool Mediterranean air from the west, which collides with the heated desert air, fierce winds and storms often occurred. Not long after the disciples had started, a strong wind began churning the sea.

¹⁹When the disciples had rowed three or four miles (about halfway across) and were out in the middle of the sea, they saw Jesus walking on the water toward them. They were terrified and scared by what they saw.

²⁰But Jesus said to them, "It is I; I am here. You do not need to be afraid."

²¹Then they gladly took Him into the boat. Even though they had only traveled about half the distance across the sea, they somehow were transported across the remaining distance and arrived immediately at

the exact destination they had set out for. During the Passover, they also celebrated a water miracle associated with Moses, but Jesus had just done a miracle that vastly surpassed any done by Moses.

²²The next day, the crowd that stayed on the other side of the sea knew there had only been one boat there the day before. They knew the disciples had left in that boat. They also knew that Jesus was not with them when they departed. ²³Then, some other boats from the seaside town of Tiberias landed. These boats landed near where the previous day's miracle occurred—where the 10,000 plus had eaten bread miraculously provided by the Lord. ²⁴The crowd was expecting Jesus and His disciples to be in these boats, as though the disciples had left just to go pick up Jesus. However, the crowd noticed that neither Jesus nor his disciples were in the boats that had arrived. So, they got into the boats and went across the sea to Capernaum searching for Jesus.

> *4.2.3 Jesus is the bread of life: Unlike manna from heaven that temporarily met people's needs, Jesus is the source of life, the satisfaction of the human heart, and the goal of God's work in the world (6:25–59).*

JESUS IDENTIFIES THAT ALL PEOPLE HAVE DEEPER SPIRITUAL NEEDS (6:25–27).

²⁵When they found Him on the other side of the sea, Jesus was at a synagogue. They said to Him, "Teacher, how in the world did You get over here?"

²⁶Jesus answered, "Let Me tell you this truth. You all are looking for Me because I gave you bread to eat and met your physical and material needs. You are not looking for Me because you paid any attention to the divine sign I offered that points you toward a deeper spiritual truth. ²⁷But do not be so focused on your immediate needs; they are like food that can perish. Look instead for a new kind of food, the food that gives a new kind of life that eternally endures. More importantly, focus not on the gift but the Giver, for it is the Son of Man who will give you this new kind of bread, because He is the One who came directly from God's presence and reveals Him to you. God the Father has put His seal of approval on the Son of Man and guaranteed what He can give you."

JESUS CALLS THEM TO TRUST FULLY IN GOD TO MEET ALL THEIR NEEDS (6:28-29)

²⁸Then they asked him, "To do what God requires of us, what should we be doing?"

²⁹Jesus replied, "This is what God wants from you: Have faith, which implies not only belief but full trust and commitment, in the One He has sent."

THE PEOPLE CANNOT IMAGINE JESUS PROVIDING FOR THEIR NEEDS MORE THAN MOSES AND ASK HIM FOR PROOF (6:30-31).

³⁰Upon hearing this, they said to Jesus, "If You really are the great prophet—the Messiah, who is the Christ—and the full treasury of heaven's provisions has been opened to us, then what miraculous sign will You show us that we may see it and believe You? ³¹After all, Moses fed our religious forefathers manna daily, and they ate that bread daily while they journeyed through the wilderness. The Scriptures in Exodus 16:4 tell us that 'Moses gave them bread from heaven to eat.' So what supernatural work will You do to prove yourself to us?"

JESUS REFOCUSES THEM NOT ON MOSES, BUT GOD; HE LETS THEM KNOW THAT GOD IS PROVIDING A NEW BREAD FROM HEAVEN TO MEET THEIR NEEDS (6:32-33).

³²Then Jesus said to them, "I am afraid you are missing the point of the Scripture. So, let Me draw your attention to this truth: It was not Moses who gave you bread from heaven. It was My Father; He is the source that gave you bread from heaven. ³³And now, there is a new and true bread from heaven that goes beyond just meeting your physical needs. God's true bread is the One who comes from heaven, the One who gives you a new kind of life with God and a new way of living to the world."

JESUS IS THE NEW SOURCE OF LIFE, GOD'S NEW BREAD FROM HEAVEN (6:34-40).

³⁴They said, "Sir, from now on give us this new bread every day."

³⁵Jesus said to them, "I am the bread that gives this new kind of life with God, the source that nourishes and satisfies existence. Whoever comes to Me will find their heart's hunger filled and never

be hungry. Whoever believes in Me will find their innermost being's thirst quenched and never be thirsty. ³⁶But the truth of the situation is the same as I told you before: You have seen Me, and yet you refuse to believe.

³⁷"But I do not worry because My work and mission depend on My Father's work. Every person whom the Father gives Me—everyone who is to experience the true bread of life—will come to Me. And whoever comes to Me, I will never reject or cast out. ³⁸For I have come down from heaven not to do My own will; I have come to do the will of Him who sent Me.

³⁹"To make the point even more clear, let Me restate what God's will is in sending Me. It is God's will that I must not lose one single person He has given Me. Why? Because when the last day comes, I will raise up all who believe in Me into the fullness of this new kind of life. ⁴⁰You see, that is what My Father wants. His will is that everyone who looks to the Son and trusts in Him will have a new kind of life, one that eternally endures. When the last day comes, I will raise up all who believe in Me and awaken them into the complete fullness of this new kind of life with God."

WHILE PEOPLE LOOK FOR EXCUSES NOT TO BELIEVE, GOD DRAWS THEM AND CALLS THEM TO TRUST IN JESUS (6:41-46).

⁴¹When the Jewish leaders heard this, they began to grumble and murmur to themselves because Jesus said, "I am the bread that came down from heaven." They recognized that Jesus was claiming that He alone was the source of life, the satisfaction of the human heart, and the goal of God's work in the world. ⁴²From their unenlightened perspective, they questioned Jesus' origin and identity, saying, "Is this not Jesus, the son of Joseph, whose father and mother we know? Coming out of a normal Jewish family, how can He possibly be saying now, 'I have come down from heaven'?"

⁴³Jesus told them, "Do not grumble and bicker with one another over Me. Besides, you are missing the bigger picture. ⁴⁴For no one can come to Me unless the Father draws them to Me. So, you do not need to bicker with each other over My identity. The Father will draw

people to Me as He sees fit, and I will raise them up into the full completeness of a new kind of life on the last day.

⁴⁵"God personally moving inside of people's hearts in this new way was envisioned in the Scriptures by the prophets. In Isaiah 54:13, it says, 'They will all be personally taught by God.' The prophet foresaw God taking the initiative to connect with His people; now, God has done just that by sending Me. And anyone who listens to the Father or learns anything from Him comes to Me. ⁴⁶For no one has seen the Father except the One who is from God. Only He has seen the Father.

JESUS' BODY IS THE SOURCE OF GOD'S NEW KIND OF LIFE, AND HE MUST BECOME A VITAL PART OF ONE'S LIFE (6:47:51).

⁴⁷"It is important that you get this, so let Me summarize this truth for you again: Whoever believes in Me receives a new kind of life that eternally endures. ⁴⁸I am the bread of life who gives you this new kind of life with God. ⁴⁹Your religious forefathers ate manna in the wilderness that sustained their lives from day to day, but it was just bread that sustained their physical needs. It did not give them a new kind of life that eternally endures, and they all still died. ⁵⁰But now there is a new bread that comes down from heaven that sustains life beyond day-to-day needs and endures throughout eternity. This new bread comes down from heaven, and anyone who eats it will never die. ⁵¹I am this new, living bread that came down from heaven. Anyone who eats this new bread will live forever in a right relationship with God. This new bread is My flesh, which I will give up as a sacrifice so that the world may have new life."

THE PEOPLE DO NOT UNDERSTAND JESUS' CLAIM AND THINK HE IS FOOLISH (6:52).

⁵²When the people heard this, they were angry at this new claim. They argued sharply among themselves, saying, "Earlier, when Jesus was saying He was the bread of life, we understood that He supposedly meant we must make a firm decision to believe in Him as God's gift of life. But with this new claim, Jesus has gone too far and apparently entered into the realm of the absurd! Now, Jesus is saying that He—His flesh, as the bread of life—will be offered up as a blood sacrifice

that will benefit the entire world. This seems ridiculous. How can this man offer up His body and give us His flesh to eat? How absurd is it that we are supposed to be cannibals who eat His flesh?"

JESUS' BODY IS THE SOURCE OF GOD'S NEW KIND OF LIFE, AND ONE MUST HAVE A FULLY CONNECTED UNION WITH JESUS TO EXPERIENCE NEW LIFE (6:53-59).

[53] Even though they were flustered by their misunderstanding, Jesus explained further, saying, "It is crucially important that you get this truth: Unless you eat the flesh of the Son of Man—the One who came directly from God's presence and reveals Him to you—and drink the blood of His sacrifice, you do not have the new kind of life that eternally endures in you. [54] Whoever feeds on My flesh and drinks the blood of My sacrifice—as their means of personally connecting to God—possesses a new kind of life that eternally endures. They experience this new kind of life partially right now, but when the last day of human history comes, I will raise them up into the full experience of the new kind of life that eternally endures.

[55] "It may seem hard to understand, but My flesh is the real food that satisfies your life's hunger; My blood is the real drink that satisfies your life's thirst—the food and drink your existence truly needs and was created to crave. [56] Whoever eats My flesh and drinks My blood experiences a union that connects them in an intimate, reciprocal relationship with Me. In this act and union, they are fully connected to and remain in Me, and I am fully connected to and remain in them.

[57] "And this fully connected union pays off to their eternal benefit! You see, God the Father lives eternally, and I live eternally as well because of My union with God the Father. Likewise, He has sent Me so that whoever feeds on Me will live eternally as well, because they have a fully connected union with Me.

[58] "During the Passover event in the Scriptures, you celebrate and remember how God provided for your spiritual forefathers by giving them bread that sustained their physical existence during the exodus journey. But that bread was only a temporary provision serving a purpose for that time. The new bread that has now come down from

heaven is different and eternally better than the old bread of the past. This new bread is the kind you were created to live off of throughout eternity. This new bread fulfills God's purpose for your lives throughout all time. I am the new bread that gives this new kind of life. Whoever feeds on Me will live forever."

⁵⁹Jesus said these things while teaching in the synagogue in Capernaum.

> 4.2.4 *Responding to Jesus: Jesus' sacrificed body is the source of life and calls everyone to make a decision about Him (6:60–71).*

WHEN PEOPLE REALIZE THAT FOLLOWING JESUS IS NOT JUST ABOUT MEETING THEIR NEEDS BUT ABOUT INGESTING GOD'S TRUTH AND TEACHING, TRUSTING IN HIM, AND DOING WHAT HE SAYS, MANY WILL TURN AWAY FROM JESUS (6:60-66).

⁶⁰When the broad group of His followers heard this teaching, many of them said, "This teaching about Jesus' identify and how He saves us is beyond difficult. It is unacceptable and beyond comprehension! How can anyone accept it?"

⁶¹But Jesus was aware that these followers were grumbling about this teaching. He said to them, "Does this teaching about the Son of Man being sacrificed and His flesh being the true bread that gives eternal life offend you? Are you incapable of seeing how His sacrifice spiritually benefits you? ⁶²If you cannot handle this talk of His death, then how will you possibly accept seeing the Son of Man ascend back into heaven again? ⁶³Your human logic, rationales, reasoning, and willpower alone are not enough to comprehend these deeper realities. The Spirit gives this new kind of life. Every word I have spoken to you is full of the Holy Spirit and the new kind of life He gives. ⁶⁴Even though I have set a new kind of life that eternally endures before you, some of you continue to resist the truth and refuse to believe." (After all, Jesus knew, from the beginning, the ones who would not believe and the one who would betray Him.)

⁶⁵Then Jesus said to them, "This is why I told you this truth earlier: No one can come to Me unless the Father has enabled them to do so."

⁶⁶After Jesus completed this teaching, it was too much for many of His followers. Many of them turned away and no longer followed Him.

JESUS' TRUE FOLLOWERS WILL ACCEPT HIS TRUTH AND TEACHING, COMMIT THEMSELVES TO FOLLOWING HIM, AND, IN CHRIST, FIND A NEW KIND OF LIFE THAT ETERNALLY ENDURES (6:67-71).

⁶⁷Then Jesus turned His attention to His smaller inner circle of twelve disciples, saying, "Do you want to turn away and leave as well?"

⁶⁸Simon Peter answered Him, "Lord, to whom would we go? There is no one else. You are the One who has the words that give a new kind of life with God, the new kind of life that eternally endures. You are the One with the words that allow us to connect to God and His kingdom. ⁶⁹We have come to trust and commit ourselves to the truth. We have learned that You are the Holy One of God—the One who is set apart from any other person in all of existence, the divine One who defends, redeems, and delivers His people."

⁷⁰Jesus replied, "Just remember: I chose all twelve of you, but do not discount the ability of the sinful nature embedded within the human will to work against God's will in your lives. Even though I chose the twelve of you, there is one among you who is a devil working directly with the Devil." ⁷¹Jesus was referring to Judas, the son of Simon Iscariot. Judas was one of the twelve disciples, but he would later turn against Jesus and betray Him.

4.3 Jesus and the Festival of Tabernacles: Jesus is the Son of God who provides those who believe in Him with an internal source of life-giving water that will never end; He is the full light of God's revelation to the world (7:1—9:41)

4.3.1 Jesus is the Christ who comes from the Father and has the authority to give life (7:1–52).

CHAPTER 7

NOT EVERYONE WILL ACCEPT JESUS AND RECOGNIZE WHO HE IS OR RESPECT HIS AUTHORITY OVER LIFE (7:1-9).

¹For a period of time after this, Jesus traveled around in Galilee. He stayed away from Judea because the Jewish religious leaders there were looking for an opportunity to kill Him. ²But several months later, the Jewish Festival of Tabernacles was approaching.

Occurring during autumn harvest, the Festival of Tabernacles was the last of three pilgrimage feasts the Jewish people celebrated each year. This festival celebrated four themes: 1) the harvest, which required farmers often to build temporary shelters (or tabernacles) in the field to store it; 2) the change in season, where prayers were made asking God to bring life-giving water to the dry land; 3) the change in light, where every day after the festival would get shorter and have less light; and 4) the faithfulness of God, praising Him for remaining true to His promise and leading the Israelites of the Old Covenant out of their wilderness period. During the festival, people often put up temporary shelters (or tabernacles) to stay in as a way of honoring the purpose and focus of the festival. The significance of the Festival of the Tabernacles cast an ever-present light in the minds of all those who attended it.

³With the time for traveling to the festival near, Jesus' brothers said to Him, "Why are You still here! You and Your disciples should leave Galilee and go to Judea. Do You not want all Your followers gathered there to see all the miraculous works that You do? ⁴You are never

going to become famous if You hide away in this secluded region. You need to go where the action is, where all the people will be gathered together. If You are serious about Your magic act and all these miraculous things, then You need to go and show them to the world." ⁵Even His own brothers did not believe in the deeper truth of who Jesus is.

⁶Jesus told them, "For a variety of reasons, now is not the right time for Me to go. But you can go anytime; you have nothing to lose. ⁷The world does not have anything against you, but it hates Me because I expose its works as evil. ⁸So, do not wait for Me. You all go on to the festival. I am not going up yet, because My time has not yet fully come." ⁹After He told them this, Jesus stayed behind in Galilee.

PEOPLE OFTEN LOOK FOR A LIGHT (OR REVELATION) FROM GOD, BUT THEY OFTEN MISS GOD'S LIGHT WHEN HE SPEAKS TO THEM (7:10-13).

¹⁰When His brothers had traveled up to the Festival of the Tabernacles, Jesus went up not too long after. He arrived discretely, staying out of public view. ¹¹At the festival, the Jewish religious leaders were already hunting for Him, asking everyone, "Where is Jesus?"

¹²Apart from their search, a buzz of excitement existed among the many people there in the crowd. They were anticipating seeing Jesus; they wondered not only what might happen when He arrived but also who He was. They whispered their speculations about who He was to each other. Some said, "He is a good man." Others claimed, "No, He is only leading people astray." ¹³But no one wanted to speak too loudly or publicly about Him, for they feared getting in trouble with the Jewish authorities.

JESUS TEACHES THAT HIS AUTHORITY COMES DIRECTLY FROM GOD THE FATHER AND MUST BE BELIEVED (7:14-24).

¹⁴Then, when the week-long Festival of the Tabernacles was about halfway over, Jesus went up to the temple and began to teach. ¹⁵The people were highly impressed by Him. They asked, "How does this man know so much when He has never had any rabbinical training or formal religious education?"

¹⁶Jesus answered them, "My teaching is not My own. It comes from God the Father who sent Me. My teaching comes directly from Him. ¹⁷Anyone who is seeking to do the will of God will be able to recognize and discern whether My teaching comes from God or whether it is merely something I have made up. ¹⁸A person speaking from their own authority and skill seeks to make themselves look good. But the one possessing a pure motive seeks to honor and show the surpassing value and worth of the One who sent Him. He speaks the truth, and there is nothing false in Him. ¹⁹Besides, has Moses not given you God's moral standards and expectations? Yet none of you are keeping them. Instead of following God's moral standard, why are you out here trying to kill Me?"

²⁰The people in the crowd replied, "Have You gone crazy or lost Your mind! Who is trying to kill You? We are not trying to kill You."

²¹Jesus answered, "I did a miracle that restored life on the Sabbath a few months ago. You all were amazed at what happened. Since then, some of you have not stopped pursuing Me and looking for a way to kill Me. They want to kill Me because they think I broke their Sabbath traditions. ²²But you all are missing the fact that you already have customs that allow you to break the Sabbath tradition yourselves. For example, Moses, in Exodus 12, gave you the law about circumcision. It dictates that you should circumcise on the eighth day (though these instructions came not from Moses but from the patriarchs). Well, sometimes that eighth day falls on a Sabbath, and you end up circumcising on the Sabbath. By circumcising on the Sabbath, you are doing work.

²³"Now, if the appointed time to circumcise a boy falls on the Sabbath, you do not hesitate to break the Sabbath law of Moses in order to circumcise him. If you are willing to break the Sabbath to do this ritual that merely symbolizes healing, then why are you angry with Me for using My divine prerogative to heal a whole man's body on the Sabbath? ²⁴You should stop judging by surface level, external appearances. Instead, use your head and your heart to judge what is true and right."

JESUS IS THE CHRIST WHO COMES FROM THE FATHER TO GIVE THOSE WHO BELIEVE IN HIM AN INTERNAL SOURCE OF LIFE-GIVING WATER SO THAT THEY WILL NEVER THIRST AGAIN (7:25–52).

> *Jesus claims that He is the Christ who comes directly from the Father, and His claim causes people to react one way or another (7:25–31).*

²⁵At this point, some of the people in Jerusalem began to ask, "Is this not the man that they are trying to kill because they say He blasphemies God? Does He not claim to be sent directly from God? ²⁶And yet here He is, speaking openly in public, and they are not saying one word to stop Him. Is it possible that these religious authorities have concluded that He really is the Messiah, who is the Christ—the One filled with God's power and authority sent to deliver His people? ²⁷But we know better than to think He is the Christ. We have a tradition that says when the Christ comes, no one will know where He is from. And we know what town Jesus is from. Since He does not meet the expectation of our tradition, He cannot be the One."

²⁸Then Jesus, who was still teaching in the temple courts, said loudly and clearly, "Yes, you know Me and My human origins. You know what town I am from while I have been on the earth. But do you really know where I come from? My true origin comes from the One who sent Me, and it seems that you do not know Him at all. ²⁹But I know Him because I am from Him. He sent Me here to you."

³⁰The crowd was split by what they heard. To many, Jesus was blaspheming God not only by claiming to have come from God but also by claiming to be equal with God. In response, they tried to arrest Him. However, no one could lay a hand on Him, because His hour had not yet come. ³¹Even though some sought to arrest Him, many others in the crowd believed in Him. They said, "When the Christ appears, do we really expect Him to perform more signs or present more convincing evidence than what Jesus has done? We have all the evidence we need to believe in Him."

The people living in the darkness of the world will reject Christ, but Jesus will return to the Father in heaven (7:32-36).

³²When the Pharisees heard that the crowds were whispering belief about Jesus, they were very alarmed. The chief priests and the Pharisees sent temple guards to arrest Jesus and to put an end to what they thought was His seditious and blasphemous heresy.

³³Then Jesus said, "These people reject Me and My teaching. So, I will only be with you a little longer, and then I will go back to the One who sent Me. ³⁴You will look for Me. You will try to figure out where I went, but you will not find Me. You cannot come where I will be."

³⁵The Jewish authorities were puzzled by what He said. They asked, "Where is He going that we will not be able to find Him? Maybe He is thinking about going out into the Gentile (non-Jewish) lands where he knows we will not go? Maybe He plans on teaching these despicable, Gentile (non-Jewish), Greek people? ³⁶Wonder what He is talking about when He says, 'You will look for Me, but you will not find Me,' and 'You cannot come where I will be'? It all seems like pure and utter nonsense."

Jesus will be a constant source of life-giving water that is freely available to all and will eternally sustain the lives of those who believe in Him (7:37-39).

³⁷The Festival of Tabernacles lasts seven days. Each day, a water ceremony takes place in which a procession of priests, followed by large crowds of people waving branches, descend the hill on Jerusalem's south border down to the Pool of Siloam. Once there, these priests fill a golden pitcher with water, and they bring it back up the hill to the temple's altar. At the temple's altar, they pour the water on it as a ceremonial act intended to honor the God who gives water in several ways. First, the water ceremony is a prayer and a plea to God for rain (since the autumn season is typically a time of drought). Second, it symbolizes how God brought water to the Old Covenant people of Israel who needed it when He had Moses strike a rock to produce water. Third, the water ceremony is also a plea to see the vision of the prophets Zechariah and Ezekiel fulfilled. They had visions of rivers of water flowing from God's temple, flowing waters that would give to

everyone in a spectacular way. Each day of the festival, these priests conducted this water ceremony. On the seventh and last day of the festival, the water ceremony and its procession took place seven times.

Within this context, on the last (and what is considered the greatest day) of the festival, Jesus stood up and said in a loud voice, "If anyone thirsts, let him come to Me and drink. ³⁸I am the new Temple and the source of living water. When struck, I will produce an eternal abundance of life-giving water that will be freely available to all. Whoever believes in Me, as the Scripture has said in Isaiah 55:1, Isaiah 58:11, Ezekiel 47, and Zechariah 14:8, 'rivers of living water will flow out from within their hearts.'"

³⁹When Jesus mentioned "living water," He was referring to the Holy Spirit who would later be given to everyone who had faith in Him. At that time, the Holy Spirit had not yet been given to believers because Jesus had not yet been raised to glory.

> *People are often divided in their response to Jesus' truth claims; Some reject Him, others believe in Him (7:40–44).*

⁴⁰When the crowds heard this saying, they had divided responses. Some people said, "Surely this man is the great prophet Moses promised would come in Deuteronomy 18:15. Surely He is the One we have been expecting."

⁴¹Others spoke with simple trust and assurance, saying, "This man is the Christ, the Messiah filled with God's power and authority who is able to deliver His people."

Yet others did not believe and said, "How can our Messiah come from Galilee? ⁴²Does the Scripture not clearly tell us that the Messiah, who is the Christ, will be born from the royal line of David and be born in Bethlehem, the town of David? We know that this man comes from Galilee, and that does not add up with what we expect."

⁴³So the crowd was divided in their beliefs about and response to Jesus. ⁴⁴Some of them even wanted to arrest Him, for they thought He was breaking the Jewish traditions, but no one laid a hand on Him.

Even religious leaders can miss out on and reject Jesus (7:45–52).

⁴⁵When the temple guards went back and reported to the chief priests and Pharisees, they asked the guards, "Why did you not arrest Him for the great disturbance He is causing with His erroneous, inconsistent teachings?"

⁴⁶The guards answered, "We have never heard anyone speak the way that this man does!"

⁴⁷The Pharisees replied, "Have you allowed Him to lead you all astray as well? ⁴⁸Have you seen any of the Jewish leaders or the Pharisees believe in Him? I do not think so! ⁴⁹But this foolish crowd that is ignorant of God's law follows Him. May God's curse be upon all of these foolish and ignorant people who are led astray."

⁵⁰Nicodemus, who had visited with Jesus earlier and who was one of these Jewish-ruling leaders, asked, ⁵¹"Does our Jewish law legally convict and condemn a man without first giving him a hearing, without first learning more about what he has been doing?"

⁵²They replied, "Have you somehow become one of his simple-minded, Galilean followers too! You should search the Scriptures more and then you would know better. When you do, you will find that no prophet ever comes out of Galilee."

[The earliest manuscripts and other ancient witnesses do not contain John 7:53–8:11]

4.3.2 While many—including religious leaders—may condemn one's sinful behaviors, Jesus offers forgiveness; He calls everyone to follow God's new way of life (7:53–8:11).

⁵³As the day passed, the crowd went home.

CHAPTER 8

¹That night, Jesus went to the Mount of Olives, which is to the east of Jerusalem and on top of a hill that overlooks the city. ²Early the next morning, Jesus went back to the temple. All the people gathered around Him, and Jesus sat down to teach them.

³Then, the Pharisees and teachers of the Jewish, Old Covenant Law [the first five books of the Old Testament] brought in a woman they had caught in adultery. They forced her to stand right in front of the group so that everyone could see her. ⁴They said to Jesus, "Teacher, according to Old Covenant Law, to accuse someone of adultery, we have to have two witnesses who catch the person in the actual act of adultery. Well, we caught this woman in the act. ⁵In the Old Covenant Law, Moses commanded us to stone every woman caught in adultery. But what do you say? What do you think we should do?" ⁶They were using this entire situation to test Jesus; they hoped to trick Jesus into a trap, hopefully finding something they could use against Him.

But Jesus did not immediately respond. Instead, Jesus bent down and began writing on the ground with His finger. ⁷When they kept on pestering Him for an answer, Jesus stood up and said to them, "Let whoever is without sin be the first one to throw a stone at her." ⁸Then Jesus bent down and wrote more on the ground.

⁹When they heard what Jesus said, they began to walk away, one right after the other. The older ones were the first to walk away; then the others left until there were no accusers remaining. Jesus was left alone with only the woman standing before Him.

¹⁰Then Jesus stood back up and asked her, "Dear woman, where did all of your accusers go? They seemed so adamant and determined a minute ago. Has no one remained to condemn you?"

¹¹She replied, "No one remained, Lord."

Jesus replied, "Then neither do I condemn you. You may go on your way, but from now on, leave behind your life of practicing sinful behaviors and living in a way that displeases God."

> 4.3.3 Jesus is God's light—His revelation—that illuminates one's life and guides them through every aspect of life (8:12-30).

JESUS IS THE LIGHT OF THE WORLD AND ILLUMINATES A PATH OUT OF THE DARKNESS OF THE WORLD (8:12-20).

¹²Jesus continued teaching them during the Festival of Tabernacles. The festival combined multiple themes from the Old Covenant's history: Celebrating the harvest, longing and praying for God's supernatural favor that would bring water to overcome the drought, remembering how God guided His people through the desert via temporary shelters (tabernacles), and focusing on the temple of God—which they believed to represent where God dwelt among them on earth—as being central to religious life.

Another key theme during the Festival of the Tabernacles was light. The festival included a vast celebration of light because it occurred during the fall equinox (which meant, until spring, there would be more darkness during the day than light). Every night of the festival, one of the most impressive sights one could see in life was displayed for all to see; it was the temple filled with and reflecting amazing light. Placed around the outer court of the temple were four large stands, each holding four huge golden bowls. These sixteen huge golden bowls were filled with oil that was lit each night. The light they produced—along with all other lamps around them—was so bright that it illuminated the entire beautiful temple. The light produced was so strong that it reflected off the temple and lit up the entire city of Jerusalem! In everyday life, with little more than small lamps to give off light personally or publicly, seeing the temple and all of Jerusalem illuminated at night was one of the most incredible sights in human existence.

During the festival, with everything in sight illuminated all around Him, Jesus talked to the people, saying, "I am the light of the world—a specific, spiritual illumination from God that reveals His plan for all existence. Whoever follows Me will never walk in darkness but will have a new kind of light illuminating and guiding their lives."

[13]When the Pharisees heard this statement, they replied, "You are making an audacious claim about Yourself. Words about Yourself and Your own self-testimony are not enough. More evidence is needed. The Jewish tradition requires at least two witnesses to corroborate a testimony for it to be valid."

[14]Jesus answered, "You are accustomed to needing two human witnesses to validate the truth. But you do not recognize that when I testify about Myself, that is all that is needed to verify the truth and its reliability. I know the place where I came from originally. I also know the place where I am going to next. But you seem to have no idea where I am from or where I am going. [15]You are judging everything by mere human standards of what you can touch, verify, and understand, but I do not make judgments on anyone like that. [16]However, if I did, My judgments would be right and correct. For I would not be making judgments from a limited perspective that lacked any knowledge, because I am not alone. The Father who sent Me is with Me, and I have a perfect union with Him. My judgments would be made with the full knowledge and complete perspective of the Father who has sent Me. [17]Even as it is written in your own Old Covenant law, the testimony of two witnesses is valid. Well, you have that right here, right now—the testimony of two witnesses! [18]I testify about Myself; there is your first witness. And God the Father who sent Me testifies about Me; there is your second."

[19]Then they asked Him, "You keep talking about Your Father. But where is Your so-called Father at?"

Jesus replied, "You understand as little about God the Father as you do about Me. If you knew Me and understood who I am, then you would also know My Father."

²⁰Jesus said all these things in the treasury area of the temple court. Since it was where the temple offering was made, it was a heavily populated area. Yet no one arrested Him, because His hour had not yet come.

THOSE WHO BELIEVE IN JESUS WILL LIVE WITH HIM AND ETERNALLY BE WHERE HE IS GOING; THOSE WHO DO NOT BELIEVE IN HIM WILL DIE IN THEIR SINS AND WILL NOT GO TO WHERE HE IS GOING (8:21-30).

²¹Then Jesus said to them again, "There is coming a time when I will leave you and go away. When I go, you (the Jewish people) will search for Me (the Messiah), but you will be missing the big picture. Even though you search for Me, you will die in your sin. Why? Because you will have missed the mark with God by not believing in the Christ, the anointed One filled with God's power and authority sent from above to decisively deliver His people. Because of your sin and your unbelief in Me, you cannot come where I am going."

²²Upon hearing this, the Jewish people wondered, "What does Jesus mean by, 'You cannot come where I am going'? Is He planning on killing Himself?"

²³Jesus said to them, "You continue to look at everything from a limited human perspective—a view from below. I am looking at things from a non-limited, divine perspective—a view from above. You continue to look at everything from a limited view because you belong to this world, but I am not of this world. ²⁴That is why I told you very plainly that you will die in your sins because you have missed the mark of God's standard for your life. If you do not believe that I AM who I say I am, you will miss God's way of salvation and die in your sins."

²⁵They asked, "If we do not believe that You are 'I am?' That sounds confusing. What do You mean by that exactly? Just tell us who You are."

Jesus replied, "I am the One who has been telling you who I am from the beginning. ²⁶I have so many more things to tell you about the sad reality that awaits you. A sad reality awaits you because of the sinful things you have done before God that deserve His holy and just condemnation. But why tell you about those things when you do not accept what you have heard from the One who sent Me? It is a shame that you do not believe, because He who sent Me is completely truthful, and I declare to the world what I have heard from Him."

²⁷They clearly did not grasp that Jesus was telling them about God the Father. ²⁸So, Jesus said to them, "When you have witnessed the series of events that lead to the glorified and lifted up Son of Man, then you will know that I AM who I say I am. Then you will know that I do and say nothing of My own authority but speak only what the Father has taught Me. ²⁹You are going to realize that the One who sent Me is always with Me. He has not left Me alone, and I always do His will and whatever pleases Him."

³⁰While Jesus was saying these things, many believed in Him.

THOSE WHO BELIEVE IN THE TRUTH OF JESUS ARE SET FREE AND BELONG TO GOD'S FAMILY; THOSE WHO DO NOT BELIEVE REMAIN IN THE SLAVERY OF THEIR SINS AND DO NOT BELONG TO GOD'S FAMILY (8:31-38).

³¹Then Jesus turned His attention to those Jewish people who claimed to believe in Him. He said, "If you remain faithful to My teachings—putting them into practice and letting them shape your life—then you are truly My disciples. ³²From first-hand experience, you will know the truth for yourselves, and the truth will set you free."

³³They were perplexed by what He had said, so they replied, "What do You mean by being 'set free'? We are the spiritual and religious descendants of Abraham. We have never been spiritually or religiously enslaved to anyone. We are already free. So why are You trying to tell us that we will be set free?"

³⁴Jesus responded, "You are missing the point. So, let Me tell you this crucially important truth: Everyone who commits and practices sin—which is anyone who misses the mark of God's standards for their

life—is a slave to sin. ³⁵As you know, slaves have no security or no permanent place within the family. However, a son born into the family has security and permanently belongs to the family. Well, the Son that God sent is a permanent part of God's family. ³⁶And if the Son, who is a permanent part of God's family, sets you free, then—like a slave released from their captivity—you are truly free indeed!

³⁷"Yes, I fully realize that you see yourselves as Abraham's descendants. Because of that, you think you have a special relationship and family connection with God. You think that historical heritage gives you spiritual freedom. However, you are missing out on God's message to His family right now. Instead of hearing Him, you are looking for a way to kill Me. You are looking to kill Me because there is no place within you for My teaching, a teaching that says how the purpose of God's family is being fulfilled through Me. ³⁸I am telling you about what I have seen in My Father's presence, but instead of listening to Me, you are doing what you have heard from your despicable, evil father—the Devil."

ONE'S RELIGIOUS HERITAGE, BACKGROUND, OR NATURE DOES NOT MAKE ONE A CHILD OF GOD; ONE MUST ACCEPT JESUS'S TEACHING AND TRUST IN HIM (8:39-47).

³⁹They were upset by this and answered, "But Abraham is our religious and spiritual father. We have a special relationship with God because of it."

Jesus said, "If you were truly Abraham's children, then you would be doing what Abraham did: trusting in God's message and His way. ⁴⁰Instead, here you are looking for a way to kill Me, trying to kill the One who has told you the truth He heard directly from God the Father. Abraham had faith in God, and what you are doing is nothing like how Abraham acted. ⁴¹You are merely continuing to do the works of your despicable, evil father—the Devil; he is your real father."

They were angered by this and said, "What are you talking about? We are not illegitimate children. We have a special relationship with God because of Abraham; God Himself is our only Father."

⁴²Jesus told them, "If God were your Father, then you would love Me. I have come directly from God, the Father, and I am the One here before you now. I did not come by My own initiative or in My own authority. God sent Me. ⁴³Why do you not understand what I am saying? Let Me tell you why. Because you are unwilling to listen to and accept My message. ⁴⁴Because of your spiritual and religious heritage, you want to think you have a privileged, special relationship with God. However, your inner being—the core of who you are—belongs to your real father, the Devil. Your will and heart are set to do your evil father's despicable will and set to follow the Devil's evil desires. From the beginning of human history, the Devil was a murderer with Cain and Abel. He has always resisted and hated the truth because there is not one ounce of truth in him. When he lies, he is merely doing what is consistent with his entire nature and character. After all, his entire being and existence are corrupt. He is a liar and the father of all lies.

⁴⁵"In case you need evidence that you are his children: I come and tell you the plain, simple truth about God. Yet, you do not believe Me. ⁴⁶You question My origin and where I came from, but the proof is right here in front of you. For example, is there anyone of you who can accuse Me of any sin, of missing the mark of God's standard's and will in any way? Of course you cannot accuse Me of any sin, because there is no sin in Me, and I have not sinned. So, if I am here telling you the truth about God, then why do you not trust and believe in Me? ⁴⁷But here is the reality of the situation: Whoever belongs to God hears and accepts what God says. The reason that you do not hear or listen to Me is because you do not belong to God."

JESUS CLAIMS THAT HE IS GOD AND EXISTED BEFORE THE WORLD WAS CREATED; PEOPLE EITHER BELIEVE THAT TRUTH OR THEY DO NOT (8:48–59).

⁴⁸Then the Jewish leaders responded to Jesus, saying, "If You think we are of the Devil because we do not listen to You, then it must be because You are one of those despicable Samaritans, those who are unacceptable before God because they are a defiled race. Maybe You are the demon-possessed one?"

⁴⁹Jesus answered, "Since you are not listening, it may seem to you like I am crazy. But I am not demon-possessed or promoting Myself in any

way. I am simply honoring God, My Father, while you are dishonoring Me. ⁵⁰I am not seeking any honor or glory for Myself, but God the Father is going to honor and glorify Me. He is the ultimate Judge, the One who will make it happen. ⁵¹I am telling you this truth, and you need to listen to it: If you keep My word and put My teachings into practice, you will have the kind of life that will never taste death!"

⁵²Then they said to Jesus, "Now we know that You are insane! Abraham died. The prophets in the Old Covenant Scriptures died. And here You are saying, 'If anyone keeps Your teaching, they will have the kind of life that will never taste death!' ⁵³Do You think You are greater than our spiritual and religious father Abraham? Or the Old Covenant prophets? What kind of selfish, crazy, self-glorification are You attempting here? Who in the world do You think You are?"

⁵⁴Jesus answered, "I am not trying to honor or glorify Myself at all. If I were seeking My own honor, it would be self-seeking and mean nothing. Instead, it is My Father who will honor and glorify Me. You like to claim that 'He is our God and we have a special relationship with Him because of our spiritual heritage.' ⁵⁵But you do not even know Him.

"While you all may not know Him, I do, and I have been trying to tell you that. If I acted like I did not have direct, personal, and complete knowledge of the Father, then I would be a worse liar than all of you. But I do know the Father, and I have a responsibility to tell you that I know Him, because I am doing what He has told Me to do. ⁵⁶You widely accept that Abraham had tremendous gifts and prophetic insight, that God had given Abraham a prophetic awareness of the day of the Messiah's arrival. Yes, your spiritual forefather had an immense joy that he would see this day, and here it is—the day of My arrival. He saw it and was glad."

⁵⁷The Jewish leaders said to Jesus, "You continue to be a religiously dangerous, crazy, and insane man! You are not even fifty years old, and yet You are saying You have seen Abraham who has been dead for almost two thousand years?"

⁵⁸Jesus answered, "Let Me tell you this truth plainly: In the Old Covenant Scriptures, God told Moses that His name was 'I Am." So, let Me be clear by making this claim about the absolute truth of My identity. Before Abraham was even born, I was around because I AM the I AM!"

⁵⁹When the people understood His claim about being God, that was it. To them, Jesus' claim was clear blasphemy against God, a crime that was to be punished by stoning the blasphemer to death. So, they picked up stones to throw at Him. However, Jesus was able to slip away from them. He left the temple before they could kill Him; His hour had not yet come.

> 4.3.4 Who is truly blind and who can really see? Jesus heals a blind man, showing His power and authority over life, and it reveals the spiritual blindness of those who do not believe in Him (9:1–41).

CHAPTER 9

JESUS HEALS THE MAN BORN BLIND (9:1-12). [THE SIXTH SIGN REVEALING A DEEPER TRUTH ABOUT GOD: HEALING THE BLIND MAN]

¹On the last day of the Festival of Tabernacles, as Jesus was walking along, He noticed a man who had been blind since birth. ²His disciples asked Jesus, "Teacher, the typical custom has been to assume a person's suffering is a direct result of someone's sinful choices. But here is a man that has been blind from birth. So, in this special case, who has chosen sin—missing the mark with God—and bears responsibility for this blind man's suffering? Is this suffering the result of the blind man's own sinful choices or the sinful choices of his parents?"

³Jesus answered, "It was not this man's sinful choices, nor the ones made by his parents. This man's suffering is not directly connected to anyone's sin. This man's blindness has happened so that the work of God might be powerfully displayed and revealed through him. ⁴While we are still in the daylight of My physical presence on earth, we must

do the works of the One who sent Me. The night is coming when My physical presence will no longer be here. When it does, the work will not carry on in the same exact way it does now. ⁵But while I am still here among you, there is an abundance of direct light that reveals God, for I am the light that illuminates the world."

⁶After saying this, Jesus spat on the ground and made a mixture from the mud and His saliva. Then, He put this mixture on the blind man's eyes. ⁷Then Jesus directed the blind man, saying, "Now go and wash in the Pool of Siloam, the same one that is the source of water used in the water ceremony during the Festival of Tabernacles." In Hebrew, siloam means "sent," and the pool was symbolic of the One who would be sent from God who would be the true source of healing. In this instance, the One who was sent from God and able to heal sent the blind man to the symbolic pool. The blind man followed Jesus' instructions. He went and washed in the pool and came back home able to see!

⁸When the man returned home, his neighbors and those who had formerly known him as a blind beggar were astonished. They asked, "Is this not the same blind man who used to sit and beg all day?"

⁹As they were trying to decide what had happened to him, some said, "Yes, this is the same man." Yet others doubted, saying, "No way; he is just someone that looks like him." Yet the entire time the former beggar and healed blind man kept telling them, "I am the same man that you know and are talking about; I am just healed now."

¹⁰Then they asked him, "How in the world did this happen? Who healed you?"

¹¹The former blind man answered, "The man called Jesus made a mud-saliva mixture and put it on my eyes. Then He told me to go to the pool of Siloam and wash. So, I did as I was instructed. I washed in the water, and now I can see."

¹²They asked, "We need to investigate this miracle worker. Do you know where he is?"

The man replied, "No, I do not know."

PEOPLE MAKE A PSEUDO-ATTEMPT TO INVESTIGATE THE REALITY OF JESUS, REFUSE TO BELIEVE THE EVIDENCE, AND REVEAL THEIR OWN SPIRITUAL BLINDNESS (9:13–23).

¹³Then the formerly blind man's neighbors and others took him to be examined by the Pharisees, the Jewish group dedicated to strictly observing the Old Covenant [Old Testament] laws and their customs around it. ¹⁴The day that Jesus opened the blind man's eyes with the mud-saliva mixture was on a Sabbath, a day when no work was allowed. ¹⁵So, the Pharisees interrogated the formerly blind man about his healing. They asked, "How did you receive your sight back?"

The formerly blind man told them, "Jesus put a mud-saliva mix on my eyes, and when I washed it off, I could see."

¹⁶When the Pharisees heard this, they had mixed responses. Some of the Pharisees said, "Well, there we have it; all the evidence we need! This man is clearly not from God because He does not keep the Sabbath tradition." But others wondered, "How can a man who is disregarding the Sabbath tradition do such amazing, God-like signs like healing this man?" An obvious division of opinion existed among them.

¹⁷Then the Pharisees continued their interrogation of the formerly blind man. They asked him, "How about yourself? What is your opinion about this man who healed you and opened your eyes?"

He said, "It seems to me that He is more than just a miracle worker. It seems that He is at least a prophet doing the works of God like the Old Covenant prophets of old did."

¹⁸The Jewish leaders of the Old Covenant were in a dilemma. They were looking for some way to dismiss what had happened. They wanted to refuse to believe that the man had been blind from birth

and had received his sight. So, they called in the formerly blind man's parents to ask them about his condition. ¹⁹They asked his parents, "Is this man really your son? Was he really born blind? If so, how can he now see?"

²⁰His parents answered, "Yes, we know that he is our son. Yes, he was born blind. ²¹But how he can see now or who opened his eyes, we do not know. We suggest you ask him. He is a grown man and can reliably speak for himself." ²²His parents answered this way because they feared the Old Covenant Jewish leadership. It was already known that these leaders had decided that if anyone acknowledged that Jesus might be the Christ, the Messiah, they would be expelled from the synagogue and all community associations. ²³That is why his parents, not wanting to risk religious and social expulsion, said, "He is a grown man; ask him."

THE FORMERLY BLIND MAN POINTS OUT THE SPIRITUAL BLINDNESS OF THOSE WHO REFUSE TO BELIEVE IN JESUS (9:24-34).

²⁴The Pharisees were still not satisfied with their investigation. So, for a second time, they summoned the man who had been born blind. They said to him, "Why are you pointing to Jesus as the man who healed you. We know only God can do that. Give God the glory that He is due by telling the truth about how you were healed. Because we know that Jesus is a sinner who openly disregards God's Sabbath and our traditions, and God cannot possibly work through someone like that."

²⁵He answered, "Whether this man is a so-called 'sinner' or not because He breaks the Sabbath tradition is not for me to know. But one thing I do know—I was blind, but now I see!"

²⁶They said to the former blind man, "Did this man somehow warp your mind as well? Tell us the truth now. What evil spell or black magic did he do to open up your eyes?"

²⁷The former blind man answered, "I have already told you how it happened, but you were not listening. Why are you so interested in

hearing it again? Do you want to become His disciples so that you can learn the ways of God from Him too?"

²⁸In response, the Pharisees hurled insults at the formerly blind man and cursed him, saying, "You must be out of your mind and be one of this man's disillusioned disciples. But not us. We are disciples who learn about God's ways from Moses. ²⁹We know with certainty that God has spoken to Moses. But this man, Jesus, we do not even know where He comes from."

³⁰The former blind man answered, "Well, it seems strange to me that you have not connected the dots yourselves. You say you do not know where this man comes from, but the plain fact and clear evidence is right in front of you—He opened my eyes to be able to see! ³¹We accept, as common knowledge, that God does not listen to sinners. We also believe that if anyone lives a life of devotion, worships God, and lives to do His will, that God eagerly listens to that person. ³²From the time the world began until now, no one has ever heard of anyone opening the eyes of a man born blind and healing him so that he can see fully and clearly again. ³³It looks crystal clear to me: If this man were not sent from God, He could not do what He has done."

³⁴The Pharisees responded to the formerly blind man: "It is now clear that you were born a complete and total sinner who is destined to miss God's mark for your life forever. You are covered in God-dishonoring sin from head to toe. And besides, who do you think you are you to take that kind of tone with us? Given who we are—our religious training, backgrounds, and positions of leadership—do you really think you have anything to teach us about God?"

JESUS REVEALS WHO IS BLIND AND WHO CAN REALLY SEE (9:35-41).

³⁵When Jesus heard that the Pharisees had cast the formerly blind man out of the synagogue, He found the former blind man and asked him, "Do you believe in the Son of Man, the One who came directly from God's presence and reveals His path of salvation?"

³⁶The former blind man answered, "Yes! Can you tell me who He is, sir? I want to believe in Him."

³⁷Jesus said to him, "You have now seen Him with your own eyes. He is the One who is speaking with you right now."

³⁸The former blind man replied, "You are my Lord, and I place all my trust in You." Then the formerly blind man worshipped Jesus.

³⁹Jesus said, "I came into this world to shine God's light onto it so that each person's true nature and motives could be called into judgment. I have brought everything into God's light, and it calls for a decision. The result of My light coming into the world: Those who have been blind will see, and those who think that they see everything clearly will become blind."

⁴⁰Some of the Pharisees were standing nearby and heard what Jesus said. They asked, "Are you trying to say that we are blind to seeing God's ways and understanding His work in the world?"

⁴¹Jesus answered, "If you were spiritually blind, you would not be guilty of sin and be blameless. However, since you claim to see everything about God so clearly, your guilt remains, and you cannot escape it."

4.4 Jesus and the Festival of Hanukkah: Jesus is the Son of God who guides and leads God's people in the way of life (10:1–39).

4.4.1 Jesus is the gate through which people gain access to God's family, and He is the Good Shepherd who knows and leads His sheep (His people) (10:1–21).

CHAPTER 10

JESUS SHARES A STORY ABOUT THE IMPORTANCE OF THE GATE TO THE SHEEP PEN AND THE GOOD SHEPHERD (10:1-6).

¹Three months had passed since the Festival of Tabernacles; it was now winter and time for the Festival of Hanukkah. The Festival of Hanukkah recalls a time when a group of Jewish fighters called the Maccabeans recaptured the temple by fighting the Greeks and Greek-minded Jews. These Jewish fighters felt that the Jewish faith—and the temple as the centerpiece of it—had been corrupted by Greek influence. Led by Judas Maccabeus, they fought to purify Judaism and to retake the temple. The temple was not only the center of the Jewish faith, but it was thought to be God's house, where His presence resided on earth. Once the Maccabeans' revolt was victorious, and they recaptured the temple, they purified it and rededicated it to God. For eight straight days, they burned oil in the temple as an act of dedication. Because of this, the Festival of Hanukkah was celebrated for eight days. And during the Festival of Hanukkah, the Jewish people reflect on the Maccabean event and examine their dedication to God.

While narratively Jesus addressed the following people with a message that picks up where He left off at the Festival of Tabernacles, chronologically, it was three months later. Also, thematically, Jesus' message was shared in the context of the Festival of Hanukkah, a time when the people asked hard questions about failed religious leadership and false shepherds who might lead them astray.

Within this context, Jesus said to them, "You all know well the structure of sheep pens. They have walls waist high that are topped with thorny branches designed to keep the sheep safe. They only have one small opening as their point of entry. The shepherd typically guards the entrance to the pen personally with his body. Knowing this structure, now let Me tell you this important truth: Anyone who does not enter the sheep pen through the gate, but climbs in by some other way, is a thief and a robber.

²"The One who enters through the gate of the sheep pen is the shepherd of the sheep. ³The gatekeeper opens the gate for him. When the shepherd goes in, he is recognized by the sheep as having a rightful place among them as their shepherd. Because of his direct and ongoing relationship with them, the sheep also recognize and listen to his voice. He knows his sheep and calls each one by name. When he calls to the sheep, they follow his familiar voice, and he leads them out to find green pastures. ⁴When he brings out all his flock of sheep, he walks in front of them, leading them along the way. The sheep follow him because they have direct knowledge of and ongoing trust in his familiar voice. ⁵However, the reverse is also true. The sheep will not follow a stranger's voice. Instead, they will turn and run away from him because they do not recognize, know, or trust the stranger's voice." ⁶Jesus told them this simple parable—a story that illustrates a deeper religious truth—but they did not understand what He meant by it.

JESUS IDENTIFIES THAT HE IS THE GATE TO ENTER GOD'S FAMILY AND THE GOOD SHEPHERD WHO GUIDES AND LEADS GOD'S PEOPLE (10:7-18).

⁷So, Jesus explained the story to them, saying, "Let Me tell you this truth even more plainly and directly. I am the gate, the One through whom access to the sheep pen can be gained. ⁸Other false shepherds (and false religious leaders) that have come before Me are thieves and robbers. But the true sheep—people desiring to follow God's voice—did not listen to them.

⁹"As I said before, I am the gate, and another aspect of Me being the gate is this: Whoever enters through Me will find safety, security, and provision. In these lands that are full of evil—where food and water

are scarce—My sheep will be saved. They will go in and come out without fear for their safety. Even though they live in a desert wilderness, they will find desirable green pastures that offer vibrant provisions for living. ¹⁰The thief (the false religious leaders) comes only to steal and kill and destroy the sheep. But I have come so that they might have a new kind of life, a life fuller and more abundant than any they have ever known or can imagine.

¹¹"In addition to being the gate, I am also the good shepherd. The good and noble shepherd sacrifices his life for the sheep. ¹²The hired hand is not like the real shepherd who does not own the sheep. When the hired hand sees trouble coming, he is more concerned about his own wellbeing. He abandons the sheep and runs away. Then, the wolf attacks the sheep and scatters them. ¹³The hired hand runs away because he is just working for the money he gets from work. He does not care about the sheep's wellbeing; he is not personally invested in them.

¹⁴"I am the good shepherd. I have a personal knowledge and union with My sheep. I know My sheep, and they know Me. ¹⁵The personal knowledge and union we share are mutual and comprehensive. It resembles the perfect union I have with the Father—where the Father knows Me, and I know My Father. My knowledge and love for My sheep are so deeply and profoundly personal that I am willing to sacrifice My life for them. ¹⁶I also have other sheep that are not of the Jewish flock. I must bring them with Me as well. They will recognize and listen to My voice. The end result: There will be one flock of God's people following One Shepherd.

¹⁷"Do you know why the Father loves Me? Because I freely and voluntarily lay down My life to serve His will, so that I can receive it back again. ¹⁸No one can take My life from Me; I am not a victim. I lay My life down voluntarily of My own free will. I have been given full authority to lay it down in sacrifice and to take it back up again. I have received this power and authority directly from My Father."

GIVEN JESUS' ABSOLUTE CLAIMS ABOUT WHO HE IS, PEOPLE ARE DRIVEN TO A RESPONSE (10:19-21).

¹⁹When Jesus said these things, it caused another divided response among the people. ²⁰Many of them said, "This Man is completely insane and has lost His mind. Why would anyone listen to His crazy talk?"

²¹But others argued, "These are not the words of a crazy, demon-possessed man. Do you not remember what He did a few months ago—healing the man born blind? Can a crazy, demon-possessed man heal and open up the eyes of a man that has been blind since birth?"

4.4.2 Jesus' claims to be the Christ, and people must make a decision about Him (10:22-39).

JESUS CLAIMS TO BE THE SON OF GOD, AND PEOPLE'S PROBLEM IS NOT THAT THEY HAVE NOT BEEN TOLD BUT THAT THEY DO NOT BELIEVE (10:22-30).

²²They continued celebrating the Festival of Hanukkah in Jerusalem, which occurs during the winter. ²³The main temple courtyard was surrounded by massive, covered colonnades on all sides. On the east side was Solomon's Colonnade. Many teachers used the porches at Solomon's Colonnade to block the cold wind and winter weather. Jesus was walking along in this area. ²⁴The people there surrounded Him and said, "How long are You going to annoy us by keeping us in all this suspense? If You are the Christ—the anointed One filled with Gods' power and authority sent to decisively deliver His people—then just tell us plainly."

²⁵Jesus answered them, "I have already told you. The problem is not that you have not been told; the problem is that you do not believe. Everything I do reflects My Father's character, power, and authority and gives you all the proof you desire. The works I have done are like a direct testimony from God about Me. ²⁶However, that is not enough for you. Simply put: You do not believe because you are not My sheep. ²⁷My sheep recognize, listen to, and respond to My voice. I have a personal connection with them, and they follow Me. ²⁸As a result of their trust and personal union with Me, I give them a new kind of life that eternally endures. They will never perish, and no one can snatch

or steal them out of My hand. They are secure. ²⁹My Father, who has given them to Me, is greater than any robber, thief, or destroyer. No one is greater than He, and no one can snatch or steal My sheep out of My Father's hand. ³⁰The Father and I are One. We are the same, and We work together in a perfect union with one another."

EVEN THOUGH THE SCRIPTURE FORETELLS THAT THE SON OF GOD WOULD COME IN HUMAN FORM, SADLY, PEOPLE STILL REJECT JESUS (10:31-39).

³¹When the Jewish people heard what Jesus had said, they considered it blasphemy. Once again, they picked up stones to kill Him for a crime punishable by death. ³²Jesus answered them, "I have shown you many good works that came directly from My Father. Which of these good acts are you going to stone and kill Me for?"

³³They replied, "We are not going to stone You for the good works You have done. We are going to stone You for Your outright blasphemy! Even though You are just a human being, You blaspheme by claiming to be equal with and the same as God!"

³⁴Jesus answered them, "Is it not written in the Old Covenant law, in Psalm 82:6, that God says, 'I say to you—you are gods.' ³⁵If the Psalmist called these lower beings who received God's message 'gods,' and if Scripture cannot be broken and does not mislead, then how are the words from a Higher Being (My words received from God) blaspheming against Him? ³⁶If Scripture is okay calling these non-divine beings 'gods,' then why are people protesting, objecting, and saying I am blaspheming if I—the One the Father sent into the world—say 'I am the Son of God'? After all, I am the One God the Father chose and set apart as His holy place; He chose My body, not the temple, to be His presence in this world. ³⁷If I am not doing the works of God the Father, then do not believe Me or put your trust in Me. ³⁸However, if I am doing the works of God, even though you find it difficult to believe My words, then at least believe in the works I have done. Then you will know and understand the direct, perfect, and personal union that the Father and I share as One—that the Father exists in union with Me, and I exist in union with the Father."

⁳⁹Once again, they tried to arrest Jesus for blasphemy, but He slipped away and escaped from their grasp.

MANY PEOPLE RECOGNIZE THAT JESUS IS THE SON OF GOD SENT TO SAVE THE WORLD AND BELIEVE IN HIM (10:40-42).

⁴⁰After the Festival of Hanukkah was over, Jesus went back across the Jordan River. He went back to the place where John the Baptist had been baptizing in earlier days. He stayed there in the desert wilderness a while. ⁴¹Many people came out to see Him and hear His teaching while He was there. They reflected on all that had happened and said, "Even though John the Baptist did not perform miraculous signs, he was a trustworthy witness to the Christ because everything he said about Jesus has come true." ⁴²And in that place, in the deserted wilderness away from Jerusalem and the so-called religious experts and leaders, many recognized God's hand in Jesus' works and God's voice in Jesus' words. As a result, many believed in Jesus.

5. Jesus reveals God's light to the world (how He will save His people), and everyone who comes to God's light will no longer live in darkness (11:1–12:50).

   5.1 Jesus demonstrates His power over life and death; yet, people plot to kill Jesus (not knowing they are actually fulfilling God's plan) (11:1–57).

   5.1.1 Jesus provides a paradigm for how God will save His people (11:1–44). [The seventh sign revealing a deeper truth about God: Raising Lazarus from the dead]

CHAPTER 11

JESUS IS TOLD THAT LAZARUS HAD DIED BUT SAYS IT WILL RESULT IN GLORY (11:1-16).

¹Some time later, after the Festival of Hanukah, a man named Lazarus was extremely ill. He lived in the town of Bethany, which was about

one and a half miles east of Jerusalem. His sisters Mary and Martha lived there too. ²This is the same Mary who later anointed the Lord's feet by pouring very expensive oil—worth nearly a year's wages—on them and wiping it away with her hair. Mary's brother was Lazarus, and he was very sick.

³So Mary and Martha sent a message to Jesus, saying, "Lord, we know that You coming to our location—to the area near Jerusalem—is a risky endeavor, because the religious leaders are out to get You. But we wanted to let You know that our brother, the one You love, is extremely sick."

⁴When Jesus heard the report, He said, "This sickness will not end in death. No, this event will be used for God's glory. The Son of God's worth and value will be recognized through it."

⁵Now Jesus loved Martha, her sister Mary, and Lazarus. ⁶However, when He heard the news that Lazarus was deathly ill, Jesus stayed where He was for two more days. ⁷After these two days had passed, then Jesus said to His disciples, "Now let us go back to Judea to visit Lazarus."

⁸The disciples said to Him, "Teacher, it was not that long ago that the Jews there wanted to stone You! And You want to go back there again?"

⁹Jesus answered, "Are there not twelve hours of daylight every day? When people walk in broad daylight, they will not stumble; the light from the sun gives this world natural light. But remember, I am the light of the world, a specific, spiritual illumination from God that reveals His plan for all existence. By walking with Me in the work that I am doing, you can be confident I will guide you through anything that comes your way. ¹⁰However, the end of the spiritual light that My presence brings to the world is approaching. The night is coming, and it brings tragedy and crisis with it. When a person walks through life surrounded by the night of spiritual darkness, with no illumination from God to guide them, they are in danger of stumbling because they have no spiritual light. But for now, the light is still here. So, let

us not worry about any darkness that we may encounter on our way to Judea."

¹¹After saying these things, Jesus said to them, "Our friend Lazarus has fallen asleep, but I am going to go there to wake him up."

¹²The disciples responded, "Lord, if he has just fallen asleep, then he will surely get some rest, recover, and be better soon."

¹³The disciples thought Jesus meant Lazarus was simply resting and sleeping. They had no clue Jesus was telling them that Lazarus had died. ¹⁴So, Jesus told them plainly, "Lazarus has died. ¹⁵While it is a sad occasion, it is to your benefit that I was not there. What you are about to see will encourage your belief and trust in Me. But now, let us go and see him."

¹⁶Then Thomas, also nicknamed Didymus (meaning the Twin) said to the rest of the disciples, "Even though going back near Jerusalem is a risky, life-threatening endeavor, let us go with Jesus and fight alongside Him if need be. If Jesus is destined to die, then we will die with Him."

JESUS TEACHES THAT THOSE WHO BELIEVE IN HIM WILL HAVE A NEW KIND OF LIFE THAT ETERNALLY ENDURES (11:17-27).

¹⁷When Jesus arrived at Bethany, He found that Lazarus had already been in the tomb for four days. Four days was significant because the Jewish people believed that the soul of a dead person remained in the body's vicinity hoping to reenter it for three days. However, once the body's decomposition started after three days, the soul departed. Also, another Jewish custom was to go to the tomb three days after the burial, to make sure the person remained dead and had not resuscitated. So, by the time Jesus arrived and Lazarus had been dead for four days, it was finally and fully accepted that Lazarus was dead.

¹⁸Bethany was only about one-and-a-half miles from Jerusalem. The people there lived very public lives; it was normal for them to have relational connections with others within the town—and even beyond the immediate community. ¹⁹As a result, many Jewish people

had come to grieve with Martha and Mary, to comfort them over their brother's death.

²⁰When Martha heard that Jesus was coming, she went out to meet Him, but Mary stayed behind in the house. ²¹Martha said to Jesus, "My dear Lord, if You had been here, I am confident that You could have healed Lazarus and that my brother would not have died. ²²But nevertheless, my faith and belief in You have not wavered. I know God works mightily through You, and You are doing the work that He has given You to do. I remain confident even now that He will give You whatever You ask."

²³Jesus said to her, "Do not worry. Your brother will rise to life again."

²⁴Martha replied, "Yes, like many faithful Jews, I am confident that at the end of time—at the resurrection that will occur among God's people—he will rise again."

²⁵Jesus said to her, "I am both the resurrection that will change everything and the new kind of life that will never end. These are not abstract things to merely hope for; they are realities that I have complete power and authority over. Those who trust in Me will live a new kind of life that surpasses death. Even if they die, they will experience this new kind of life that overcomes death. ²⁶Everyone who believes and continues to live in Me will never really die anyway. Do you believe this?"

²⁷She responded to Him, "Yes, Lord. I believe You are the Christ, the Messiah who has this kind of power and authority over life and death. I believe You are the Son of God who has come into the world to decisively deliver and save His people."

> **JESUS WEEPS OVER DEATH, WHICH IS AN UNWELCOME INTRUDER ON GOD'S CREATION (11:28–37).**

²⁸After Martha had said this, she went back and talked to her sister, Mary. She told Mary privately, "The Teacher is here. He is looking for you."

²⁹When Mary heard this news, she rose to her feet and quickly went to Him. ³⁰Because Jesus' presence near Jerusalem might cause a dangerous riot, Jesus stayed in a small village nearby, just outside the town of Bethany (the same place where Martha had met Him previously). ³¹Inside Mary's home, many Jewish people were there to console and mourn with her. When they saw Mary stand up and leave quickly, they assumed she was going to the tomb to pour out her grief there.

³²When Mary arrived at the place where Jesus was staying, she saw Him and fell down at His feet. She said, "Lord, if You had been here during Lazarus' illness, then my brother would not have died."

³³In society, public grieving with loud, public displays of grief was normal. Yet when Jesus saw Mary loudly wailing and crying, and saw the large crowd of people loudly weeping too, deep anger and outrage sprang up from within Him. In His inner being, Jesus felt the emotion of the scene and was moved by it. Even though He was present as the resurrection and the life, He was deeply troubled by the sad situation of death and its effects.

³⁴Jesus asked, "Where have you laid his body?"

They replied, "Lord, come, and we will show You."

³⁵Full of sadness and feeling deep anger at death and the devastation it brings, Jesus wept.

³⁶The audience was divided on what to make of Jesus' weeping. Some of the Jewish people said, "Look how deeply He loved Lazarus!" ³⁷While others were more cynical, saying, "If Jesus loved him so much, then why did He not do something about it? He opened the eyes of the man born blind. Why did Jesus not act to keep Lazarus, the 'one He loved,' from dying?"

JESUS DEMONSTRATES HIS POWER AND AUTHORITY OVER DEATH BY RAISING LAZARUS FROM THE DEAD (11:38-44).

³⁸Then Jesus, feeling deep anger at death and the devastation it brings, came to Lazarus' tomb. The tomb, like many in that region, was a

hollowed-out cave in a hillside. As was custom, it had a large stone that could be rolled away across its entrance. ³⁹Jesus said, "Move that stone; roll it away."

Martha, the dead man's sister, said, "But Lord, Lazarus has been dead for four days. His body will have started to decompose. If we open the tomb, there will be a terrible smell."

⁴⁰Jesus said to her, "Remember what I said. Did I not tell you that if you believed, you would see the glory—the full value and worth—of God?"

⁴¹So, they rolled the stone away from the entrance. Then Jesus lifted His eyes to the skies above, as though toward heaven, and prayed, "Father, I am thankful that You listen to Me. ⁴²I know You always hear Me, but I say all this out loud publicly right now for the benefit of the people standing here. I want them to hear, see, and believe that You sent Me, that it is You who is working through Me."

⁴³Then, Jesus called out loudly with a voice of pure and raw authority, "Lazarus, come out of the tomb."

⁴⁴Then, the dead man came out of the tomb. Lazarus' hands and feet were still wrapped with strips of the linen he had been buried in. Even his face was still wrapped with a cloth. Jesus told them, "Take these grave clothes and wrappings off him, and let him go."

> 5.1.2 Even though Jesus has demonstrated His power over life and death, people still refuse to believe in Jesus and plot to kill Him (11:45-57).

⁴⁵Once again, the result of Jesus' action—even raising someone from the dead—divided the people. Many of the Jewish people there, those who had come to support Mary during her time of mourning, saw what Jesus did, and they believed in Him. ⁴⁶However, others did not believe. They went and told the Pharisees—the Jewish group dedicated to strictly observing the Old Covenant [Old Testament] laws

and customs—what Jesus had done (and they also hoped that the Pharisees could explain away what they had seen Jesus do).

⁴⁷When they heard this news about Jesus, the chief priests and the Pharisees called together a meeting of the Sanhedrin (which was a Jewish, religious council that decided all important matters). They asked, "What are we going to do about this man? He keeps on performing many miraculous signs. He keeps on doing the kinds of things that only God can do. ⁴⁸If we let Him go on like this, everyone will believe He is the Messiah—the anointed One filled with God's power and authority sent to decisively deliver His people. Worse, if we let this commotion keep going, it will cause a big political and social uprising. When it does, the Romans will come and use their power to put a stop to it, since they care about maintaining peace under their rule and like to squash any uprisings. And if the Romans come to squash the uprising, they will destroy our temple and our Jewish way of life."

⁴⁹Then Caiaphas, the one who was High Priest that year, said, "Why do you all carry on with all of this foolish talk? What needs to happen is obvious. ⁵⁰Do you not realize that it is better for you that one man dies for the good of the people than for the entire nation to be destroyed?"

⁵¹Even though he did not realize it, the High Priest did not think or say these words on his own. As the High Priest that year, all year long, he had been prophesying that Jesus' death would be for the good of the entire nation. ⁵²He also said that the impact of His death would be so powerful that it would unite and bring together all the children of God who are scattered around the world.

⁵³So, from that day on, the Pharisees made plans to kill Jesus. ⁵⁴As a result of this formalized threat, Jesus stopped His public ministry. He no longer traveled publicly among the people of Judea. Instead, He left the area of Judea. He went to the region near the desert wilderness, to a town called Ephraim. Jesus stayed there with His disciples.

⁵⁵When it was almost time again for the Jewish Passover, many people from all over the country went up to Jerusalem. They arrived there a day early so that they could go and be ceremonially washed, which allowed them to be ritually cleansed and purified before the Passover began. ⁵⁶While there, the people kept looking for Jesus. As they stood in the temple courts, they asked one another, "What do you think Jesus will do when He arrives? Do you think He will even show up for the Passover Festival or not?" ⁵⁷While the people wondered, behind the scenes, the chief priests and Pharisees had already given the orders. If anyone knew or found out where Jesus was, they were to report it to them so that they could arrest Jesus.

5.2 Jesus is anointed for death (and His coming victory), and He enters Jerusalem to fulfill God's plan—offering people salvation through His death and resurrection (12:1–50).

5.2.1 Jesus is anointed by Mary for His death and coming victory (12:1–11).

CHAPTER 12

¹Six days before the Passover, Jesus came to Bethany, where Lazarus, the man He had raised from the dead, lived. Bethany was just one-and-a-half miles from Jerusalem, and in the area of Judea where the Old-Covenant, Jewish religious leaders were out to get Jesus. ²At Lazarus' home, they prepared a dinner to be given in Jesus' honor. Martha served the meal, and Lazarus reclined at the table with Jesus. ³Then, Mary come over to Jesus. She took a pound of a pure, expensive perfume called nard and poured it out on Jesus' feet. She used it as a way of anointing Jesus as their special, honored guest. Then, she used her hair to wipe off the oil from Jesus' feet. The sweet smell of the perfume's fragrance filled the entire house.

⁴However, one of the disciples, Judas Iscariot—the one who was about to betray Jesus—objected to this extravagant waste of money

and resources. He said, ⁵"This expensive perfume was worth an entire year's wages. Why on earth did we allow her to waste it? We could have taken the perfume, sold it, and had lots of money to give to the poor." ⁶Judas said this not because he cared about the poor. He said it because he was the treasurer of the group and kept up with the group's money. Also, Judas was a thief, as he helped himself to the money bag whenever he wanted. If the perfume had been sold, he would have embezzled some of the money from its sale.

⁷Jesus said, "Do not question the woman's motives. Sure, she could have done something else with this valuable perfume. But it was intended that she should keep it and use it in preparation for the day of My burial. ⁸You will always have the poor among you; that is not unusual. However, you will not always have My physical presence here among you; this is unique."

⁹When word got out that Jesus had arrived in Bethany, a large crowd of people came to see Him and Lazarus (whom Jesus had raised from the dead). ¹⁰The chief priests decided they would need to kill Lazarus as well. ¹¹Because of Lazarus' witness to Jesus, too many Jewish people were leaving their Old-Covenant approach to God and believing in Jesus' new way of being right with God.

> 5.2.2 Even though people celebrate Jesus' triumphal entry into Jerusalem like He's a military victor, Jesus demonstrates that His victory will be achieved as a sacrificial servant (12:12-19).

¹²The next day, the Sunday before Passover, the news that Jesus was on His way to Jerusalem swept through the city. During the week of Passover, the population in Jerusalem multiplied drastically. Over 100,000 people were in the crowd. Because of what Jesus had done the past three years, they were anticipating and expecting the arrival of their Christ, their Messiah.

¹³From their perspective, the Messiah would be a political warrior who would overthrow all worldly forces and establish an enduring kingdom in Jerusalem. Thinking that Jesus fit their view of the Messiah,

the crowd wanted to give Jesus a welcome fit for a triumphal king arriving back to the city. When a victorious military figure entered a city, people often celebrated with a grand, royal processional. In anticipation of Jesus' coming political and military victory, the Jewish crowd took palm branches to honor Him. Palm branches had been used during the Maccabean revolt over a century earlier when the temple was purified and rededicated. They became a symbol of the Jewish nation and their desire for ruling power. As Jesus approached the city, the crowd took these palm branches and went out to welcome Him. The entire crowd welcomed Jesus as their soon-to-be triumphal military king.

As they did, they shouted out,

"'Hosanna!' (which was an Aramaic word meaning 'Save us!').
Divinely favored is He who comes in the character and power
  of the Lord!
Divinely favored is the King of Israel!"

They praised Jesus because they thought they were welcoming their coming national liberator (which was their view of the Messiah).

[14]In an attempt to calm their fervor and clear up their misunderstanding, Jesus communicated a different message to them about the coming Messiah. Jesus found a young donkey and rode it into the city. Through this act, Jesus was sharing with them a different image of the Messiah. Jesus was telling them that the Messiah is a gentle, humble king who would bring peace to all nations. The Messiah, who is the Christ, would not triumph through military conquest but through the gift of a new kind of life. Jesus was showing how He fulfills this image from Zechariah 9:10, where it says,

[15]"Do not be afraid, beloved city of Zion, beloved people of Jerusalem.
Your king is coming,
Riding not on a war horse but on a young, peaceful donkey."

[16]In that moment, Jesus' disciples did not understand the symbolism. It was not until after Jesus entered into His full glory that they

remembered what had happened. Then, they realized how Jesus was fulfilling what had been written in the Scriptures about Him and that they had done these things to Him.

[17] The crowd that had been with Jesus when He raised Lazarus from the dead was actively spreading the word of what they had seen Jesus do. [18] Because they were actively telling others about this divine sign, the intrigue about Him grew. Many more people went out to meet Jesus. [19] The Pharisees said to one another, "What are we supposed to do now? This has gotten out of control. Look, the entire world is following after Him!"

> 5.2.3 Jesus tells His disciples what is about to happen, but they do not fully understand it yet (12:20–36).

[20] Among this big crowd, there were some Greeks—which refers to the non-Jewish Gentiles—who had admired the Jewish faith. They also traveled to Jerusalem from all over the world to worship during the Passover Festival. [21] These Greeks approached Jesus' disciple Phillip because he had a Greek name and was from the Greek region of Bethsaida in Galilee. They asked him, "Sir, we are interested in seeing Jesus. Can we see Him?" [22] Phillip went and told Andrew about it. Then, they both went and told Jesus about the request.

[23] Jesus answered them, "The hour has come for the Son of Man—the One who came directly from God's presence and reveals Him to you—to be glorified. The hour has come for the whole world to see His full value and worth. [24] Let Me tell you this truth: Unless a grain of wheat is buried in the ground and dies, it remains only a single seed. But if it dies and is buried in the ground, it rises up and produces much fruit. [25] In the same way, whoever loves their life in this world will lose their it. But whoever does not make life in this world their central and most important focus will have a new kind of life that eternally endures. [26] If anyone wants to serve Me, then they must follow My example. When they follow My example, and when we share the same unity of purpose, they can be confident that where I am, they—My servants—will be there with Me. They can also be confident that My Father will honor anyone who serves Me.

²⁷"But right now, My soul is deeply and terribly troubled. What should I say at the appointed hour of suffering approaches? Should I say, 'Father save Me from this hour?' No, I should not. It was for this very reason and purpose that I came to this hour. ²⁸Instead, as this appointed hour has arrived, I will say, 'Father, may others see the all-surpassing value and worth of who You are!'"

Then a Voice spoke from the skies above, "I have already shown the value and worth of who I am to the entire world, and I am about to do so again."

²⁹After the crowd heard the Voice, they were divided on what or who it was. Some explained it away as just thunder. Others said an angel was speaking to Jesus.

³⁰Jesus responded to them, "The voice you heard was not for My benefit, but for yours. ³¹The time of this world's trial has come to an end. The final verdict and judgment on this world is now being passed. Satan, the ruler of this world, will be cast out. ³²And when I am lifted up from the earth, and the verdict is final, I will draw all people to Myself." ³³In saying this, Jesus was indicating what kind of death He was going to die.

³⁴The crowd was puzzled and confused by what Jesus was telling them. They responded to Him, "We have heard from the Old Covenant Law that the Messiah—the anointed One filled with Gods' power and authority sent to decisively deliver His people and establish His kingdom—would live forever. But You are talking about the Messiah dying. So, how can You say these contradictory things, that the Son of Man must be lifted up? Who is this Son of Man anyway?"

³⁵Jesus answered them, "The light of God's physical presence in this world will shine among you for a little while longer. Choose to walk in the light while you still have the light, before the darkness overtakes you. If you choose to walk in the darkness, you will not be able to see, and you will not be able to tell where you are going. ³⁶While you still have an opportunity to make a choice, put your trust in the light of God. By doing so, you will become children of the light."

When He had finished speaking, Jesus left and hid in a secluded place away from the masses.

> 5.2.4 Sadly, too many people persist in their unbelief, having closed their eyes, minds, and hearts to Jesus (12:37–43).

³⁷Jesus had performed many signs in front of the people. He did these signs so that they would see and know God. Yet they still did not place their trust and refused to believe in Him. ³⁸This fulfilled what was foretold in Isaiah 53:1, where the words of the Old Covenant prophet Isaiah said,

"Lord, who has believed our message?
To whom has the powerful arm of the Lord been revealed?"

³⁹While Isaiah's words foretell that many people would choose not to believe in Jesus, he also tells us why they could not believe in Isaiah 6:10, where he said,

⁴⁰"The Lord has blinded their eyes, and
He has closed their mind and hardened their hearts.
As a result, they cannot see with their eyes,
Nor understand with their minds or hearts,
Nor turn from their sinful ways and back to Me,
So that I could heal them."

⁴¹Isaiah said these things because he saw Jesus' all-surpassing value and worth, and he foretold these things about Him.

⁴²Even though many did not trust in Jesus, many others did believe in Him, including a considerable number of the Old-Covenant Jewish leadership. However, these Jewish leaders would not openly admit their belief in Jesus for fear that they would be expelled from the synagogue and social connections with the Jewish community. ⁴³Unfortunately, they loved and valued human praise more than they valued the praise and approval that comes from God.

5.2.5 Jesus makes one final public plea with the people He came to save, letting them know that those who believe will be saved and those who do not will be judged and condemned (12:44–50).

⁴⁴Then Jesus made one final public plea with the people, summarizing for them what was at stake, when He said, "Whoever places their trust in Me is believing in the One who sent Me. ⁴⁵Whoever sees Me is also looking at the One who sent Me. ⁴⁶I have come into this world as a special light, revealing God to it so that whoever believes in Me shall not remain in darkness.

⁴⁷"If anyone hears My words and My teaching and does not keep them, I do not judge that person. I have not come to judge, condemn, or pass a sentence on people. I have come to save the world from these things. ⁴⁸However, everyone who rejects Me and does not accept My words needs to realize that they already have a judge. The very words that I have spoken will be their judge and convict them when the last day comes. ⁴⁹You must remember that what I have taught you, I have not spoken just from My own desires or thoughts. The Father who sent Me directed and commanded Me on what to say and how to say it. ⁵⁰And I know that His commands—His guidelines on living—are the instructions for a new kind of life that eternally endures. So, recognize that everything that I have told you is what the Father told Me to say."

THE BOOK OF GLORY (13:1—20:29)

6. Believing in Jesus is just the starting point of a life with God; one must continue to trust in Him (13:1—17:26).

    6.1 Jesus provides an example to follow (13:1–30).

       6.1.1 Those who believe should follow Jesus's example and serve others (13:1-20).

CHAPTER 13

JESUS DEMONSTRATES A MODEL OF HUMBLE SERVICE (13:1-11).

¹It was almost time for the Passover Festival, and Jesus knew that His hour had come, the hour for Him to leave this world and return to His Father. Having loved His disciples during His entire public ministry, Jesus continued to love them all the way to the end.

²Jesus and His disciples were at the evening meal. The Devil had already planted the idea of betraying Jesus into the heart and mind of Judas Iscariot, the son of Simon. ³Jesus knew the Father had given Him power and authority over all things; Jesus knew He had come from God and was going back to Him. ⁴Knowing who He was, Jesus had the courage to teach His disciples what was coming and wanted to model an example to leave with them. So, Jesus got up from the table, took off His second, outer layer of clothing, and wrapped a towel around His waist, positioning Himself just like a servant or slave would.

⁵Then Jesus poured water into a basin and began to wash the disciples' feet, drying them with the towel He had wrapped around Himself. In a day when people wore sandals on dry, dirt covered roads, peoples' feet were often dirty and in need of cleaning as they came into a house. This act of washing someone's feet was seen as degrading and

a task for the lowest in society. Only on rare occasions would someone like a child or student wash their parent's or teacher's feet, and when they did, it was viewed as an extreme act of devotion. Those of a higher social status never washed the feet of those who were below them, taking on the posture of a servant or slave who merely served others. Yet this is exactly what Jesus was doing.

⁶When Jesus came to Simon Peter, Peter asked Him, "Lord, You are of much higher status than us. Are You really going to wash my feet? You should not be doing this. I do not know why You are."

⁷Jesus answered, "What I am doing you do not understand right now, but later on, you will understand why I am doing it."

⁸Peter replied, "This is unacceptable. You are higher than us; you should never wash my feet."

Jesus answered, "I am afraid you do not understand. If I do not wash you, then you will have no part of Me or what I am doing. If I do not wash you, then you will not belong to Me."

⁹Simon Peter replied, "I do not fully understand it, but if You say this footwashing is what determines that I belong to You, then do not stop with my feet, but wash my hands and my head as well!"

¹⁰Jesus said, "I see your logic. You think that more washing will somehow give you a deeper connection with Me. However, once your whole body has been cleansed from a bath, you are clean. You do not need to be cleansed again. Just a touch up to rinse the dirt off your feet is all you need, because your whole body is already clean. And you, My disciples, are already clean all over. Well, all of you except one." ¹¹Jesus already knew who was going to betray Him. That is why He said one of them was not clean.

JESUS CALLS HIS DISCIPLES TO FOLLOW HIS EXAMPLE AND TO SERVE OTHERS HUMBLY (13:12-20).

¹²After He had finished washing their feet, Jesus put on His outer garment again and went back to His place at the table. He said to the

disciples, "Do you understand what I have done for you? To be sure you do, let Me explain it. ¹³You often call Me 'Teacher' and 'Lord.' You are right in calling Me that because that is who I am. ¹⁴And if I am your Lord and Teacher (a person typically assumed to be of higher status) and have washed your feet (a task that is typically done by someone of lower status), what does that mean for you? It means that you should always be willing to wash one another's feet; you should always be willing to treat others as though they are of a higher status than yourself; you should always be willing to serve one another. ¹⁵I have done this to set an example for you to follow. By following My example—this attitude and pattern for living—you will be doing things the same way that I have done them. ¹⁶Remember this truth I am telling you: A servant is not greater than His master, nor is a messenger more important than the one who sent him. ¹⁷If you understand these things that I am telling you, you will be filled with divine joy when you do them and put them into practice.

¹⁸"I realize that what I say does not refer to all of you, for I know the ones whom I have chosen. But this fulfills the Scripture of Psalm 41:9 that says, 'The one who eats bread with Me has betrayed Me by turning his heel's position against Me.' ¹⁹I am telling you all of this before it happens, so that when it does occur, it will reinforce everything else I have said and done, and so that you will believe that I am the great 'I Am'). ²⁰Remember this truth I am telling you as you go out: Whoever receives anyone I send also welcomes Me, and whoever receives Me also welcomes the One who sent Me."

> *6.1.2 Those who believe must persist in following Jesus' light because the darkness of the night is coming (13:21–30).*

²¹After Jesus had said these things, He was deeply and terribly troubled in His inner being. He testified to them, "Let Me tell you this truth: One of you is going to betray Me."

²²When the disciples heard this, they were puzzled. They looked around at each other and wondered who in the world He was talking about. ²³One of His disciples (the one known as 'the one whom Jesus loved') was reclining next to Him at the table, which was a common

posture during a meal. ²⁴Simon Peter prodded this disciple to ask Jesus who He was talking about.

²⁵So, the disciple leaned over to Jesus and asked, "Lord, can You tell me who it is You are talking about?"

²⁶Jesus answered, "It is the one to whom I will give bread after I have dipped it into the bowl." Then, as was very common during a meal (or when trying to honor someone), Jesus dipped a piece of bread in the bowl and gave it to each person there, including Judas, the son of Simon Iscariot.

²⁷As soon as Judas had taken the bread, Satan's progressive influence and work within his life solidified, and he fully entered into Judas. Then Jesus said to him, "What you are going to do, go and do it quickly." ²⁸ But no one at the table understood what Jesus meant and why He had given Judas those instructions. ²⁹Since Judas was the group's treasurer and kept up with all their money, some thought Jesus was simply telling him to go and buy whatever food was needed for the Passover Festival—or that Jesus was directing him to go and give a gift to the poor, which was a nighttime tradition to do before Passover.

³⁰After Judas had eaten the bread, he left immediately. And the darkness of the night had come.

6.2 Jesus gives a teaching to follow (13:31–17:26).

6.2.1 Believers will be tested when Jesus departs this world, but He will provide for their needs when He is gone through the Holy Spirit (13:31–14:31).

BELIEVERS WILL BE TESTED WHEN JESUS IS GONE (13:31–38).

Jesus leaves a new command and gives the world a way to test who His believers are (13:31–35).

³¹After Judas had left, Jesus said, "Now, the Son of Man—the One who came directly from God's presence and reveals Him to you—is

glorified; His value and worth will be seen. Now, God receives glory through the Son of Man. ³²Since God receives reciprocal glory and is glorified in the Son, God will radiate and reveal His glory through Him; God will display His all-surpassing value and worth for all to see through the Son. And God will bring the Son of Man into the fullness of His glory very soon.

³³"My dear children who are learning from Me, I am only going to be with you a little bit longer. You are going to look for Me, but just as I told the Jewish crowds earlier, I will now tell you the same thing: 'Where I am going you cannot come yet.'

³⁴"So, let Me leave you with a new command—direct instructions from Me that should guide and define your character and actions in your new kind of life with God. The new command is this: Love one another. But I am not talking about just any kind of generic love. Instead, follow My pattern and example. In the same way that I have loved you, you should love one another. ³⁵This is how everyone in the world is going to know that you are My disciples—if you love one another in the same way I did."

> *Believers can overestimate their ability to follow Jesus consistently (13:36–38).*

³⁶Simon Peter asked Jesus, "Lord, where are You going that we cannot come?"

Jesus answered, "Where I am going, you cannot follow Me there right now. But later, you will be able to follow Me there."

³⁷Peter responded to Him, "But Lord, why can I not follow You there now? I am ready to go anywhere and do anything for You. If needed, I will even lay down my life for You."

³⁸Jesus answered, "Is that right? Are you really ready to die for Me? Let Me tell you this sad reality: Before the rooster crows tomorrow morning, you will deny three times that you even know Me."

CHAPTER 14

THROUGH THE HOLY SPIRIT, JESUS PROVIDES FOR HIS DISCIPLES' NEEDS WHEN HE IS GONE (14:1-31).

Jesus is preparing a place for believers in the spiritual realm where God is, and one day soon, they will join Him there (14:1-4).

¹Jesus said, "Do not let your hearts be troubled by these things. No matter what comes, trust in God, and trust also in Me! ²Here is great news: For everyone who trusts in Me, there is a place in God's house for you. There are enough rooms for everyone in My Father's house—a room for everyone who believes. If that was not the true reality of the situation, why would I tell you that I am going away to prepare a place for you? If it were not true, I would just be uttering complete nonsense. But it is true, and I am going to prepare a place for you there. ³And if I am going away to prepare a place for you, then you can be absolutely confident that I will come back and take you to be with Me so that you can always live in the place where I am. ⁴Thankfully, you all already know the way—the road that leads you to the place where I am going."

Jesus states that He is the way, the truth, and life; no one comes to the Father except through Him (14:5-14).

⁵Thomas said to Jesus, "Lord, I am afraid we have no idea where You are going, so how can we know the way to get there?"

⁶Jesus said to him, "I am the way, and the truth, and the life—the one true way to a new kind of life with God. No one comes to the Father except through Me. For without the way, there is no going; without the truth, there is no knowing; and without the life, there is no living. ⁷If you have a deep, personal knowledge of Me, then you will also have a deep, personal knowledge of My Father. But from now on, you do know Him, and you have seen Him!"

⁸Phillip replied, "Lord, we would love to see Him. Show us the Father. Just seeing a glimpse of Him will be more than enough for us."

⁹Jesus replied, "Have I been here with you all of this time, Phillip, and yet you still do not know who I am? It is very simple—whoever has seen Me has seen the Father. So, how can you say, 'Show us the Father' when you have seen Me? ¹⁰Do you not believe that I am the authorized agent sent directly by the Father, that He is the One I perfectly represent? The Father and I share such a perfect union that the words I speak to you are not of My own initiative or authority. Instead, through Our perfect union, it is the Father who lives in Me and who works in the world through Me. ¹¹Believe Me when I say that I am in perfect union with the Father, and the Father is in perfect union with Me. If that seems like too much to believe, then look at the divine works I have been done. They speak for themselves and reveal the perfect union the Father and I have.

> *When Jesus is gone, He will provide the Holy Spirit to His believers to continue His work in the world (14:12-17).*

¹²"Let Me tell you this truth: Whoever trusts in Me will not only continue doing the works I have been doing, but they will do even greater works than what has already been done. How is this possible? Because I am going to the Father, and My presence in this world will no longer be limited to this body. And these works will be 'greater' because every person who believes in Me will be filled with My Spirit. Multiplied through many and embodied wherever they go, they will be empowered to do the acts of humility, service, and love in the same way that I would.

¹³"As a result of My close relationship with you who believe, we will be able to listen to each other. I will hear your voice. Whatever you ask for that is line with who I am and My work in the world, I will do. By giving you these things that are in line with My character and work, the Father will be seen, known, and valued through the Son who gives you these things. ¹⁴You can rest assured that I will be listening. Ask Me for anything that is in line with who I am and what I am doing in the world, and I will do it!"

¹⁵Jesus continued, "If you truly love Me, then you will keep My teaching and follow My commandments, My direct instructions on how

to live in your new life with God. ¹⁶If you do, then I will ask the Father to give you help. He will give you an internal, spiritual Guide who will supply My presence within you during My physical absence. This internal, spiritual Guide will be your spiritual advocate, helping you through the trials of life. And He will be with you forever! ¹⁷This internal, spiritual Guide is the Holy Spirit who will lead you into all truth. The godless cannot receive Him, because they are not looking for Him. The world not oriented toward living for God does not recognize His existence or authority over life; they do not know Him when they see Him. But it is not that way with you. You know Him, for He lives with you, and He will be living within you.

Believers can rest assured that Jesus will come back one day soon for them, and then they will be able to exist in perfect union with God (14:18–24).

¹⁸"You can rest assured that even though I am going away, I will not abandon you or you leave you all alone. My dear little children, you will not be orphans. I am coming back to be with you. ¹⁹Yet, in just a little while, the world will see Me no longer. But it will not be long before you see Me again. Because I live, you will continue to live too.

²⁰When that day comes, when I come back to you, you will fully and finally realize that I am one with My Father. You will realize that we share a unique and perfect union. But you will also realize not only that the Father and I have a special oneness and union, but you and I do as well. You will be personally united to Me, and I will be personally united to and living within you. ²¹Our amazing, personal dynamic will be seen and known in this way: Whoever has My teaching and commandments and keeps them—putting them into practice—are the ones who love Me. They will have a profound spiritual union with God that is beyond comprehension, for whoever loves Me will also be loved by My Father, and I, too, will love them and reveal Myself to them."

²²The other disciple named Judas (not Judas Iscariot) said, "Lord, why are You going to reveal Yourself only to those who follow You? Why not show and prove Yourself to the entire world?"

²³Jesus answered, "It is not about proving Myself to the entire world. Instead, it is about people making a free choice to have a personal, dynamic, and ongoing relationship with Me. If anyone loves Me, they will keep My words and follow My teaching. In mutual fashion, My Father will love them, and We will come to them and make Our house—Our dwelling place on earth—within them.

²⁴However, the reverse is also true. If anyone does not love Me, they will not keep My words or follow My teaching. Remember, the message that you are hearing is not My own. I am giving you the message that the Father sent Me here to share. The choice to not follow Me or My teaching is a choice to reject God and not know Him.

> Once Jesus has ascended to heaven and is no longer physically present in the world, believers can be confident that the Holy Spirit will guide them in truth and life (14:25–31).

²⁵"I am telling you all of this while I am still with you so that you will have a better understanding for the time period when I am no longer with you physically. ²⁶But the internal, spiritual Guide—the Holy Spirit, whom the Father will send to be My active presence and representative working in the world—will teach you everything you need to know. The Holy Spirit will teach you about what I have done; He will remind you of everything I have told you.

²⁷"I am leaving you with an amazing gift: peace! I am leaving you with a peace that is holistic, a peace that will captivate your mind, capture your heart, and fill your soul! It is My peace (the peace of God), and I am giving it to you. Realize that I am not giving you a false hope or a false promise. I am not just saying nice things to make you feel better in the moment like the world might do. Nor am I giving you something temporary. No, I am leaving you with a permanent gift, giving you a deep, rich, soul-level peace. So, do not be troubled or afraid of what is to come, because you have My peace, the peace of God living with you.

²⁸"You have heard Me say that 'I am going away, and I am coming back to you.' Even though that may seem like a loss, if your knowledge and

love for Me were not partial at the moment, you would rejoice and be glad that I am going back to the Father. The Father is the originator of My mission, and He is greater than I. With My mission almost complete, I am excited to be going back to Him.

[29]"Again, I have told you all these things before they happen, so that when they do, they will confirm and deepen your belief in Me. [30]I will not be talking with you much longer in this physical body. The ruler of this world is approaching with his evil schemes. However, realize that he has no power over Me. [31]Instead, realize that I am voluntarily doing what the Father has commanded Me. I am doing it so that the world will know I love the Father and because I only do exactly what He has instructed Me to do.

"Come now, let us rise up and leave this place."

> 6.2.2 *Believers must remain vitally connected to the source of this new kind of life (15:1–17).*

CHAPTER 15

JESUS, AS THE VINE, IS THE SOURCE OF GOD'S NEW KIND OF LIFE; BELIEVERS ARE BRANCHES THAT MUST REMAIN VITALLY CONNECTED TO HIM, THE VINE (15:1-11).

[1]"Do you recall how the vine imagery is used in the passages of the Old Covenant [Old Testament] to describe Israel? The vine imagery represented how Israel was God's specially chosen people. God had chosen them, planted them, nurtured them—including pruning them when necessary—so that they may produce the fruit of faithfulness in the world for Him. However, the people of Old-Covenant Israel were often unfaithful, disconnected, and separated from God. They did not live up to the vine symbolism, and they failed to produce faithful fruit for God. Now, let Me introduce you to a new understanding using the same Old-Covenant imagery.

"I am the true vine that produces the fruit of faithfulness for God in the world, and God's people must be connected to Me in order to live; My Father is the gardener. ²He cuts off every branch of Mine that does not produce the fruit of faithfulness. Every branch that does produce fruit, He prunes and trims so that nothing can hold it back from producing more fruit.

³"Because of your trust in Me and the message I have shared, you have already been pruned—trimmed and cleaned—to produce more fruit. And this pruning work is a good thing because it prepares you for more faithful fruit production for God. However, to be fruitful, ⁴you must remain vitally connected to Me, and I will remain vitally connected to you. No branch can produce fruit disconnected from the life-giving vine. It must remain connected to the life-giving source of the vine. In the same way, you cannot produce fruit for God unless you remain connected to Me.

⁵"I am the vine; you are the branches. Whoever remains vitally connected to Me, I will remain vitally connected to them. They will produce much fruit that is pleasing to God. But apart from Me, you cannot produce the kind of fruit God desires of you. ⁶If anyone does not remain vitally connected to Me, that person is like a broken-off branch that is thrown away. Cut off from the life-giving source, these broken-off branches wither and die. Then, they are gathered up and thrown into the fire and burned. ⁷But if you remain in Me and My words are a vital source of life within you, then ask for anything you want. If you are vitally connected to Me in this way, then your request will be like what I would ask for, and then it will be done for you. ⁸The goal is that you should produce and bear much fruit for God. When you do, it puts the Father's value and worth on display for others to see and proves to everyone that you are My disciples.

⁹"As the Father has loved Me, I have loved you in the same manner. Now, it is your responsibility to remain vitally and continuously connected to My love. ¹⁰How can you know if you are remaining in My love? If you keep My teaching and commands—following My direct instructions on how to live the new kind of life with God—then you remain vitally connected in My love. This relational dynamic works the same way with the Father and Me as well. I have kept His commands and done all that He wanted Me to do, and I remain vitally

connected to His love. ¹¹I have told you how to stay connected to God's love so that the fullness of joy that I have may be in you, and so that you may have the fullest joy possible in life, not lacking anything.

SHARING THE SAME VINE AND SOURCE OF LIFE, BELIEVERS (AS BRANCHES CONNECTED TO THE VINE) SHOULD PRODUCE FRUIT THAT REFLECTS GOD'S CHARACTER TO THE WORLD (15:12-17).

¹²"What is the essence of My teaching and My instructions for you on how to live? It is this: Love one another in the same way that I have loved you. ¹³There is no greater way to love someone than to lay down one's life for one's friends. ¹⁴And you are My friends if you do what I command you to do.

¹⁵"I no longer call you 'servants,' because a servant does not know what the master is doing. But now, I call you 'friends,' because everything I have heard from the Father I have disclosed and shared with you. ¹⁶Remember, you did not choose Me, but I chose you. I put you in the world so that you would produce fruit for God, fruit that will endure. When your character has been changed to look like Mine, then whatever you ask the Father for, He will give you. ¹⁷So remember, the command that you are to follow—the essence of My teaching and My instructions on how to live—is this: Love one another.

> 6.2.3 *Believers will live and face challenges in the world, but the Holy Spirit will help them to thrive for God through it all (15:18-16:33).*

THE WORLD WILL BE SET AGAINST BELIEVERS (15:18-16:4A).

¹⁸"But as My friends, those who embody My character and love in this world, remember how the world has responded to Me—and be encouraged by it! If the godless world hates you, remember that it first hated Me. ¹⁹If your beliefs, character, and actions were the same as the unbelieving world's, it would love you as if you were one of its own. However, your beliefs, character, and actions are not the same as the unbelieving world's. You do not belong to it. Instead, I have chosen you to come out from the godless world, to be set apart from it and for God. The result: The world is going to hate you for the godly, faithful life you will live.

[20]"Remember what I taught you: 'A servant is not greater than his master.' If they have persecuted Me—the Son of God—then you can expect that they will persecute you too. Likewise, for those who listen to My message and obey it, they will listen to your message and obey it as well. [21]Unfortunately, the people of this world are going to persecute you because of Me. They will persecute you because your life embodies and reflects My life, and because they do not know the One who sent Me.

[22]"However, the reality is that these people, like everyone else, are accountable for their spiritual condition because of God's revelation to the world. If I had not spoken to them, they would not have been guilty of missing the mark of God's standard to such a large degree. But since they now know God's truth, they have no excuse for missing the mark with God. [23]Their attitude toward you is also indicative of how they are missing the mark with God, for whoever hates you also hates Me. And whoever hates Me also hates God the Father. [24]If I had not done these signs and divine works among them, they would not have been guilty of missing the mark of God's standard to such a large degree. But the reality is this: Even though they have seen these signs and divine works, they not only rejected them but also ended up hating both My Father and Me. [25]This was bound to happen, as it fulfills what is written in their own Old Covenant law, in the Psalms, where it says, 'They hated me for no valid reason.'

[26]"But when the internal spiritual Guide comes—the Spirit of truth sent to you from the Father to continue My presence and work in the world—He will testify and confirm the truth about Me. [27]It is also your responsibility to testify and confirm the truth about Me as well because you have been with Me and have seen and heard everything I have done from the beginning of My public ministry."

CHAPTER 16

[1]"I have told you all these things to keep you from falling and from going astray when you encounter difficulties ahead. [2]And rest assured, rough times will come. People will expel you from your past religious

connections (at the synagogue) and from their community. Indeed, the hour is coming when whoever kills you will think they are doing a good service for God. ³They will do these things out of ignorance, because they have not known the Father or Me. ⁴But remember, I have told you these things now so that when the time of persecution comes, you will recall that I warned you about them in advance.

THE HOLY SPIRIT WILL GUIDE BELIEVERS TO OVERCOME THE WORLD'S CHALLENGES (16:4B-33).

The Holy Spirit works within the world (16:4b-15).

"I did not tell you these things earlier, because I knew I was going to be physically present with you for a while. During that time, I wanted you to focus on what we were doing. ⁵But now, I am going back to the One who sent Me. Even though I have told you about the coming persecution and My going away, none of you are curious about My destination. You are not asking Me, 'Can You describe to us and tell us about the place where You are going?' ⁶Instead, what I have said has filled your hearts with sadness because you have been focused on the wrong subject—your grief (over what you might lose) rather My destination (what you will one day gain).

⁷"But let Me tell you this truth: Even though you may not fully understand it now, it is to your benefit that I am going away. When I go away, I will send the Holy Spirit—the internal spiritual Guide—to come and be in a close, personal, and dynamic relationship with you. If I do not go away, then He will not come and be with you. ⁸When He comes, the Holy Spirit will prove to the people of the world the truth about their sin (how they are missing the mark with God), about their righteousness (how they can be brought into a right relationship with God), and about their decision-making and judgments (how they determine what is good and bad, right and wrong).

⁹"First, the Holy Spirit will convict the people of the world how they miss the mark with God because they refuse to believe in Me. They like to think that by refusing Me they are doing the right thing in the world, but this error causes them to miss God's mark for their lives. The Holy Spirit will lead them away from their unbelief and toward faith.

¹⁰"Second, the Holy Spirit will convict the people of the world about what right living is and about how to be right with God. They like to think that everything they are doing is right and that they can figure out their own way to be right with God. But this error causes them not to be right with Him. The Holy Spirit will lead them to turn away from trusting in themselves and toward realizing that being right with God comes through Me, and from My going to the Father (when you can no longer see Me as you do now).

¹¹"Third, the Holy Spirit will convict the people of the world about how they make decisions and judgments. They like to think that they are making a correct judgment by convicting and condemning Me and My teaching; they fail to realize that Satan, the ruler of this world, has led them astray. But this error leads them toward the same divine judgment and eternal condemnation that awaits Satan. The Holy Spirit will lead them to turn away from faulty decisions and toward realizing that the correct judgment happened when Satan, the ruler of this world, was condemned.

¹²"I have so much more that I want to say to you, but it is more than you can handle right now. ¹³But do not worry. Our conversation and your growth and learning will continue. When the Spirit of truth—the Holy Spirit—comes, He will guide you into all truth. You can trust what He says because He does not and will not speak of His own authority. The Holy Spirit will speak only what He hears from the Father. He will help you to see and better understand the new things that are to come in the future, all of which will be fully in line with everything you have heard Me say and seen Me do. ¹⁴The Holy Spirit's purpose is to honor Me. He will accomplish this purpose by helping you to know My all-surpassing worth and value, and by making known to you what He has heard from Me. ¹⁵The Father, Son, and Holy Spirit—We all have a special, unique, and perfect union. All that the Father has is mine. That is why I said, 'The Spirit will tell you whatever He receives from Me.'

> *Even though Jesus will depart from His disciples for a little while, soon He will return, and their sadness will be turned into joy (16:16–24).*

[16]"In a little while, you will not see Me anymore. But, in just a little while after that, you will see Me again."

[17]When the disciples heard this saying, they said to one another, "What is He talking about? What does Jesus mean by saying, 'In a little while, you will not see Me anymore. But, in just a little while after that, you will see Me again?' That makes no sense. Neither do these words that Jesus said: 'I am going to the Father.' That does not fit with our expectation of the Messiah, who is the Christ. [18]And now that we are thinking about it, what does Jesus mean by 'in a little while' anyway? We do not understand."

[19]Jesus could tell they were eager to ask Him about it. He said to them, "I can tell you all are curious and trying to figure out what I meant by saying 'In a little while, you will not see Me anymore. But, in just a little while after that, you will see Me again.' [20]So, let Me tell you this truth: Something is about to happen that will cause two totally different responses and experiences in people. Their beliefs about God and whether they trust in Him will determine their response to and experiences related to what is about to happen. You—as My followers—are going to weep and deeply mourn, but the unbelieving people of the world will be glad and joyful. However, even though you will grieve soon, your grieving will not last. Soon, your grief and deep sorrow will be transformed into a lasting joy.

[21]"Let Me share this analogy with you so that you will have some idea of what it will be like. When a woman is about to give birth, she experiences pain because her hour has come. However, after the baby has been delivered, she no longer remembers the pain or anguish. Instead, she experiences pure joy because her child has been born into the world. [22]This is similar to how it will be with you. Now is the time of your grief, distress, and sorrow. However, I will see you again, and then your hearts will be full of joy, and no one will be able to take your joy away from you.

²³"When that day comes and I am with you again, you will be so filled by the joy of our relationship and the knowledge that comes with it that you will no longer be full of questions. Let Me tell you this truth: The time is coming soon when whatever you ask of the Father that is in line with who I am and what I am doing in the world, He will give it to you. ²⁴I realize that you have not prayed in this manner before. But the time is coming soon when you can ask for anything in My name—anything consistent with My character and work in the world—and you will receive it. When you do, you will be filled with an overwhelming and overflowing joy!

> *Believers can be confident that Jesus has overcome the world and that He will empower His followers with His peace while they live in it (16:25-33).*

²⁵"I have told you these things indirectly through parables and in figures of speech. But the hour is coming when I will no longer talk with you through figurative language. I will tell you things about the Father very clearly, plainly, and directly. ²⁶When that day comes, there will be a new kind of relationship between all of us. I will not need to continue making requests to the Father on your behalf. Instead, in prayer and through living a life that is consistent with My teaching, you will be able to ask God the Father directly for whatever you want! You can be completely confident that He will listen to you. ²⁷The Father Himself will have a special love relationship with you because you have committed yourselves to love Me and have believed that I came directly from Him.

²⁸"To summarize, let Me speak clearly, plainly, and directly with you now about My mission. My origins are divine; I came from the Father. My mission has been known; I was sent into the world to reveal God to it. And now, My work is almost complete; I am going back to be with the Father."

²⁹His disciples responded, "Finally! At last, You are speaking clearly and plainly with us without all these figures of speech. ³⁰We can see now that You know all things. You can answer a question before it is even asked! So, You do not have to worry about us asking any more questions. We get it, and we are convinced. We trust that You came from God."

³¹Jesus said, "Really? Do you truly think you have it all figured out now, and that you fully believe and completely trust in Me? ³²Sadly, the hour is coming—and indeed is now here—when you will run away and scatter in every direction. Each one of you will abandon Me; each of you will hide in your homes. Even though you will abandon Me and will leave Me alone, I will not be alone at all because My Father is with Me. ³³I have told you all these things so that you may find and have peace in Me. In this world, you will have trouble, but be courageous and never lose heart, for I have defeated and overcome the world!"

> 6.2.4 Jesus prays for His disciples to reflect His character and to demonstrate His value and worth as they live in the world (17:1–26).

CHAPTER 17

JESUS PRAYS THAT GOD'S ALL-SURPASSING WORTH AND VALUE WOULD BE KNOWN AS THE HOUR HAS COME FOR HIM TO COMPLETE THE WORK HE WAS SENT TO DO (17:1–8).

¹After He said these things, Jesus lifted His eyes toward heaven and prayed, "Father, the hour has come that encompasses the events leading to My departure. Because of Our unique Oneness and perfect union, when people see My value and worth, they also see Yours. So, Father, during this hour that encompasses these events, and since You have chosen to accomplish Your work in the world through Me, glorify Your Son—put His all-surpassing worth on display—so that the Son can give glory to You (and display Your all-surpassing greatness, value and worth). ²You have given the Son power and authority over the entire human race so that the Son could provide a new kind of life—one that eternally endures with You—to each person You have given to Him. ³This is the new life: To learn to know You through a deep, personal, and dynamic relationship, growing in experiential knowledge of the only real and true God and Jesus Christ, the One You have sent.

⁴"During My time on earth, I have shown Your all-surpassing value and worth, Your glory, by completing the work You gave Me to do. ⁵So now, Father, display Your glory through Me as I return to Your presence. Father, give Me the glory I had with You before the world began.

⁶"I have revealed what You are like to the ones You gave Me, the ones You set apart from the world. They belonged to You, and You gave them to Me. They have kept Your words of instruction. ⁷Now they know that everything You have given Me came from You. ⁸I have given them the teaching, the message, that You gave Me to give them, and they have accepted it. They have come to know with certainty that I truly came from You, and they have believed—entrusting their lives to the reality and fact that You sent Me.

JESUS PRAYS THAT HIS FOLLOWERS WILL REFLECT HIS CHARACTER TO THE WORLD AS THEY CONTINUE HIS WORK IN IT (17:9-19).

⁹"Father, I want to pray for these disciples who are following Me right now—the ones You have given Me while I have been on earth. Right now, I am not praying for the unbelieving world, but for those You have given Me, because they are Yours and belong to You. ¹⁰Since We exist in a perfect union as One, everything that is Mine is Yours, and all that You have is Mine. Likewise, even though at this moment I share an imperfect union with My followers that is affected by their sinful nature, as they follow Me and as My life is increasingly reflected in them, they will display My value and worth to the world and bring glory to Me.

¹¹"And now, the time has come when My physical body and presence will no longer be visible in the world. They are going to need Your help to remain united. I am coming back to You, but they will continue on, living in the world. Holy Father—the One who is set apart from every other being and above all things—protect them by the power of My life and character that lives in them as they follow Me. You gave Me this teaching, these signs, and this life as a model to give them. As they follow Me and are filled with My power and character, may it not only protect them but also keep them united with one another. May they be so united that they all seem to share one

heart, one mind, and one spirit. ¹²While I was with them, I protected them. I kept them safe as they were learning the life You gave Me to give them. Not one of them has been lost, except the son of destruction, who never really belonged to Me and was lost so that the Old Covenant Scripture would be fulfilled.

¹³"But now, I am coming back to You. I pray these things while I am still physically present in this world for their benefit. I want them to hear the joy of My obedience to You so that they may follow My example and have the full measure of My joy inside them. ¹⁴They are going to need Your strength when I am gone. I have given them Your word—the teaching, signs, and model of life You wanted them to have. Because they follow Your Word, the world has hated them, for their lives no longer reflect the character that comes from an unbelieving world, just as My life did not reflect the values and perspective of the unbelieving world.

¹⁵"I am not asking that You take them out of the world to escape its struggles or troubles. I am asking that You protect them from the Evil One, the Devil. ¹⁶After all, as these disciples remain vitally connected to Me and live life as I would, they do not belong to this world any more than I do. ¹⁷They are going to need Your help to remain holy, living a life that embodies a character set apart from the world to serve You. Make them holy by consecrating them through Your truth; Your word is truth.

¹⁸"In the same way that You have sent Me into the world with a purpose, I have sent them out into the unbelieving world with a mission. ¹⁹For their sake, I have given all of Myself (and am making Myself ready even now) to serve the mission You have given Me. I have done this—and am doing it—so that they may be made holy through the truth and consecrated by it to fulfill their purpose in this world.

JESUS PRAYS THAT ALL HIS FUTURE FOLLOWERS WOULD REMAIN UNITED IN HIM, REFLECT HIS CHARACTER, AND CONTINUE HIS WORK IN THE WORLD (17:20-26).

²⁰"Father, I am praying not only for these disciples with Me right now but also for all of those who will believe in Me through their

teaching and testimony. ²¹First and foremost, I pray that every one of them will be so united with one another that they seem to share one heart, one mind, and one spirit. Father, You and I share a mystical, perfect union; You are in Me, and I am in You. I pray that they can be united—realizing they are members of the same family—and be one in Us. As they are one in Us, their unity will help the unbelieving world. It will help them to see Me living in and through them, so that the world may believe You have sent Me.

²²"I have given My followers the same glory You have given Me to display for the word. I have done this so that Your entire family of faith may be one just as We are one. ²³I will be in them, and You will be in Me. As a result of this spiritual dynamic, they may become perfectly united and completely one. When this happens, the world will see that You sent Me; they will know You have loved Your people in the same way You have loved Me.

²⁴"Father, I want My followers to be filled with the bigger vision of the true, eternal glory they will share with Me. I want them to be right there with Me, to be right where I am so that they can see and know, experience and enjoy the fullness of My glory—the glory You gave Me because you loved Me before the world was created.

²⁵"Father, You are the One who sees all things correctly and who has perfect judgment. Even though the world does not know You, has failed to recognize You, and has refused to believe in You, I know You. And My followers know that You have sent Me. ²⁶I have made You known to them—Your way, Your truth, and Your life—and I will continue to make Your character known to them. Then, as they grow in the knowledge of You, they will have the same love that You have for Me in them, and I will live in them and fill every aspect of their lives in every way."

7. Jesus reveals God's path to redemption through His crucifixion, death, and resurrection (18:1—20:29).

   7.1 Conviction: Jesus is arrested and shows that His way is not through military revolution but through sacrificial service and sharing the truth (18:1–19:16).

   7.1.1 Jesus is arrested and shows that His way is not through a forceful revolt (18:1–11).

CHAPTER 18

¹When Jesus had finished praying, He left with His disciples, and they crossed the Kidron Valley (a ravine that separated the city of Jerusalem from the Mount of Olives). Since it was the evening of Passover, the custom was to stay near the city. There was an olive grove on the other side of the valley, and Jesus and the disciples went there.

²Judas, who betrayed Him, also knew the place; Jesus often met there with His disciples. ³So Judas led a large detachment of soldiers—along with some officers from the chief priests and Pharisees—to the olive grove. They came prepared for a war carrying torches, lanterns, and weapons.

⁴Then Jesus, knowing all that was going to happen to Him, went out to meet them. He asked, "Who is it that you are looking for?"

⁵Judas, who betrayed Jesus, was standing there beside the large group, when they answered, "Jesus of Nazareth."

Alluding to the divine name for God in the Old Covenant [Old Testament] Scriptures, Jesus said to them, "I AM He." ⁶When Jesus said, "I AM He," a holy fear for God came upon them; they all stepped back and lay face down on the ground.

⁷Then Jesus asked them again, "Who is it that you are looking for?"

They replied, "Jesus of Nazareth."

⁸Jesus answered, "I have identified Myself to you and told you that I AM He. Since I am the One you want, let all these other people go." ⁹He did this to fulfill His own statement about protecting His disciples earlier, when He said, "I have not lost a single one of those You have given Me."

¹⁰Then Peter, who had a sword—and was thinking that Jesus' glorification would be won through military battle and victory–drew it out. He struck the High Priest's servant on the ear with it, cutting off his right ear. The servant's name was Malchus, which means "my king."

¹¹Jesus corrected Peter: "Put your sword back into its sheath. My glory will not be displayed in this way; it will be shown through another means. Should I not drink the cup of suffering the Father has given Me?"

> 7.1.2 The religious leaders put Jesus on trial for claiming to be God; they convict Him of a crime punishable by death (18:12–27).

JESUS IS TAKEN TO STAND TRIAL BEFORE ANNAS, THE FORMER HIGH PRIEST (18:12-14).

¹²Then the Roman soldiers, along with their commanding officer and the Jewish temple guards, arrested Jesus. They bound Him ¹³and took Him to Annas, who was an influential former High Priest, the highest-ranking one among them. Even though Annas was a former High Priest, the Jewish people believed these appointments were for life. So, they still referred to Annas by the title of High Priest. Annas was also the father-in-law of Caiaphas, who was the Roman appointed High Priest for that year. (While the Romans allowed many religious freedoms, they officially chose the High Priest each year as a means of maintaining their control over the Jewish people.) ¹⁴Caiaphas was the one who had advised the Sanhedrin—the Jewish ruling council—that it would be best if one man died on behalf of all the people.

PETER DENIES JESUS FOR THE FIRST TIME (18:15-18).

¹⁵As they were taking Jesus to Annas, the High Priest, Simon Peter and another of Jesus' disciples were following them. This other disciple knew the High Priest. So, he was able to enter the High Priest's courtyard along with Jesus, ¹⁶but Peter had to stay outside by the gate. The other disciple, being known by the High Priest, went back and spoke to the servant girl who managed the gate entrance. Then, he brought Peter inside.

¹⁷As he was coming in, the servant girl said to Peter, "You are not one of Jesus' disciples, are you?"

Peter replied, "No, I am not."

¹⁸Since it was cold, the servants and officers made a charcoal fire and were standing around it to keep warm. Peter was also standing there with them, warming himself by the fire.

JESUS IS QUESTIONED BY THE HIGH PRIEST, BUT ANNAS AND THE JEWISH RULING COUNCIL LACKS THE AUTHORITY TO PUT JESUS TO DEATH (18:19-24).

¹⁹While Peter was being questioned outside, inside, Annas, the High Priest interrogated Jesus about His disciples and His teaching. ²⁰Jesus answered, "I have always spoken openly in public for the whole world to hear. I have always taught in synagogues or at the temple, where the Jews all come together to hear religious teaching. I have said nothing in secret. ²¹So why do you question Me in private about what I have taught like I am a false prophet trying to entice people or deceive them secretly? I have taught others openly and publicly. If you would give Me a proper public trial or follow normal judicial procedure, you would be able to ask anyone who has heard My teaching. Why not ask them? They would tell you what I have said."

²²When one of the temple guards heard what Jesus said, he thought Jesus was being rude to the High Priest. So, he slapped Jesus across the face and said, "How dare you talk like that to the High Priest! You should address him with more respect."

²³Jesus answered, "If I have said something wrong about the proper and normal judicial procedure, then tell Me what was wrong. However, if what I have said is right and true, then why did you hit Me?"

²⁴Annas saw that his line of interrogation was not producing the desired result. So, he had Jesus bound and sent Him to Caiaphas. Caiaphas was the current High Priest who would have the appointed authority—religiously, with the Sanhedrin, and politically, from his friendship with Pilate—to make something substantial happen.

PETER DENIES JESUS FOR THE SECOND AND THIRD TIME (18:25-27).

²⁵Meanwhile, outside, Simon Peter was still standing by the fire trying to keep himself warm. The others around the fire asked, "You are not one of Jesus' disciples, are you?"

Peter denied it, saying, "No, I am not."

²⁶Then one of the High Priest's servants, one who was a relative of the man whose ear Peter had cut off, asked, "Did I not see you at the olive grove with Jesus?"

²⁷For the third time, Peter denied knowing Jesus. At that moment, a rooster crowed, just as Jesus said it would.

> 7.1.3 *The Roman trial: Jesus is brought to stand trial before the Romans because they have the power to put Jesus to death for a capital offense. (18:28-19:16).*

JESUS STANDS TRIAL BEFORE PILATE (18:28-40).

²⁸In the early morning hours, after Jesus' trial with Caiaphas had ended, they led Jesus from Caiaphas' house to the Roman governor's palace. However, these Jewish religious leaders did not go inside, because coming into contact with a non-Jewish person might make them ceremonially unclean. And they wanted to ensure that they would not miss any of the many meals celebrated during the Passover season.

²⁹So, Pilate came out to them and said, "What charges are you bringing against this man?"

³⁰They replied, "If this man were not a notorious evildoer, we would not have brought Him to you?"

³¹Pilate said, "Evildoer—that sounds like a religious and moral case. Take Him and judge Him according to your own religious law."

But the Jews said to Pilate, "Due to Roman law, we do not have the power to execute those guilty of capital offenses. Only Roman civil authorities have that power. This man has claimed to be our king, which makes Him a political revolutionary guilty of inciting rebellion against Rome. That is why we brought Him to you." ³²This happened to fulfill what Jesus had said about what kind of death He was going to die.

³³Since the charge of being a rebellious, political revolutionary was a capital offense, the case now fell under Pilate's authority as governor. So, Pilate decided to conduct a formal inquiry. Pilate went back into his palace and asked that Jesus be brought to him. Pilate said to Jesus, "Let's get to the point: Are you the King of the Jews?"

³⁴Jesus answered, "That sounds like a religious question instead of a civil or political one. Is this your own personal question because you want to know My real identity, or did others feed you this question to set Me up as some kind of seditionist or political revolutionary set against Roman rule?"

³⁵Pilate replied, "Am I a Jew? Do I look like I am interested in a theological debate? Your own people and chief priests brought You here to stand trial for a capital crime. They have claimed that You say You are a king. I must investigate the charge and uncover what that means, to see if You are a revolutionary, terrorist, or any type of threat to Roman rule and peace. So, now, tell me, what have You done wrong? If You are a king as they claim, is Your kingdom a threat to peace?"

³⁶Jesus answered, "My kingdom is not of this world. If My kingdom were of this world, My servants would have already been up in arms and fought to prevent My arrest. But notice, they have not behaved like that, for My kingdom is of a character—a power and authority—that is not of this world."

³⁷Pilate said to Him, "So, You are saying that You are some kind of king then?"

Jesus answered, "You are the one saying I am a king. My purpose here is far more important than titles. The reason I was born and the reason I came into this world is to testify to the truth. Everyone who cares at all about the truth hears My voice and listens to Me."

³⁸Pilate replied, "What is truth anyway?"

After saying this, Pilate went back outside to the Jews again. He said to them, "I find no guilt in this man or anything else wrong with Him. ³⁹But it is customary that I should release one prisoner to you each year during Passover. So, what would you like for me to do? Do you want me to pardon Jesus and release 'the King of the Jews' to you?"

⁴⁰They shouted back, "No! Not Him! Give us Barabbas instead!" Barabbas was an overly zealous, religious guerilla warrior who, in open rebellion, thought he could take down Rome; he was one whom Rome had already convicted as a terrorist. Yet the Jewish religious leaders preferred that a rebellious terrorist and genuine threat to Rome be released to them instead of Jesus.

CHAPTER 19

JESUS SENTENCED TO DEATH (19:1-19:16).

¹Since the crowd was determined, Pilate ordered Jesus to be flogged. Roman law had different levels of flogging. This first flogging of Jesus was their lowest level, which was intended to be a strong and severe enough punishment that it would adequately remind one never to

commit the crime again. So, in an attempt to appease and satisfy the crowd, Pilate ordered that Jesus be taken away and flogged at this first level (for Jesus' first flogging). ²To mock Jesus' kingly status, the Roman soldiers twisted together a crown of thorns and put it on His head. They also clothed Jesus with a pseudo-purple robe to mimic a purple robe, like one that a king might wear. ³The soldiers came up to Jesus, repeatedly mocking Him with insults, saying, "All hail the so-called king of the Jews!" They also hit Him in the face.

⁴After this first flogging was over, Pilate brought Jesus out to the crowd again and said to them, "Look, I am about to bring a beaten Jesus out here to you. But I want to let you know that I find no basis for your charges against Him. Nonetheless, I have had Him severely punished on your behalf. He is in bad shape from the beatings and will bear the marks of His punishment for a long time. They will be a warning for Him to never again do the horrible things you think He has done."

⁵Then Jesus was brought out wearing the crown of thorns and the pseudo-purple robe. Pilate said to them, "Just look at this bloody and beaten man!"

⁶When the chief priests and the temple guards saw Him, they were not satisfied because He was still alive. They shouted, "Crucify Him! Crucify Him!"

Pilate responded, "If you want to crucify Him, take Him and do it yourselves. Because I do not find this man guilty of a capital crime deserving of death."

⁷The Jewish leaders replied, "We have a religious law against blasphemy. According to that law, Jesus ought to die, because He has claimed to be the Son of God, meaning one who has God's full authority. Under Roman law, we do not have the authority to kill Him, or we would. So, we have brought Him here that you might uphold the local law, which is the Roman custom."

⁸When Pilate heard that Jesus had claimed to divine, Pilate was even more afraid of the events that were unfolding. ⁹He decided to dig

deeper into his formal investigation. He took Jesus back inside his palace and continued the interrogation. Pilate said to Jesus, "Where did You come from? Are You a divine man?"

Jesus did not answer his question.

¹⁰Pilate asked, "Why do You refuse to speak to me? Do You not realize that I have the power to release You and the authority to have you crucified?"

¹¹Jesus answered him, "You would have no power or authority over Me unless it had been given to you from God above. Those who have betrayed Me and handed Me over to you have missed the mark with God and are guilty to a greater degree than anyone else."

¹²From that point forward, Pilate anxiously tried to find a way to release Jesus and set Him free. However, the Jewish leaders kept shouting, "If you let this man go, you are not keeping local law, which is the Roman custom. If you let him go, you are no friend of Caesar. If you are not a friend of Caesar's, then you are Caesar's enemy. Anyone who claims to be a king is a rebellious threat to Caesar and opposes the Roman Emperor's rule. This man deserves to be killed!"

¹³When Pilate heard this, he worried about his own future if he did not appease the crowd. Tiberius Caesar had a reputation for eliminating any internal Roman governor who opposed him or allowed rebellion to occur in any way. So, Pilate brought Jesus out to stand before them again. Pilate sat down on the judgment seat where Roman trial verdicts were made. The place was known as the Stone Pavement, which in Aramaic is the word Gabbatha. ¹⁴It was around noon on the day of Preparation during Passover week, which occurred on Friday, the day before the Sabbath. Pilate said to the Jews, "Look at this bloody and beaten man! Does He look like a political or military threat to you?"

¹⁵But they shouted back, "Kill Him! Execute Him! Crucify Him!"

Pilate asked, "But is He not your king? Must I crucify your king?"

The chief priests showed just how far their hearts were from God in their reply when they said, "We have no king except Caesar!"

¹⁶ªFinally, Pilate relented. He delivered Jesus over to them to be crucified.

7.2 Crucifixion: Jesus, the Son of God, gives His life for the world (19:17–42).

¹⁶ᵇSo the soldiers took charge of Jesus. To prepare Him for crucifixion, the soldiers led Jesus out to receive the highest level of flogging (the one often used in death sentences, which used spikes at the end of the whip to ensure flesh was ripped open or away with each strike).

7.2.1 Crucified: Jesus fulfills God's plan and is crucified on behalf of the world (19:17–27).

¹⁷Carrying His own wooden cross beam on His shoulders, Jesus went out to the place called "the Place of the Skull," which in the Aramaic is called Golgotha. ¹⁸There, they crucified Jesus. They crucified Him alongside two convicted terrorists (just like Barabbas, who was released) who were a threat to Rome. One convicted terrorist was crucified on each side of Him; Jesus was crucified in the middle, between them.

¹⁹When a person was crucified by the Romans, a sign listing the person's crime was often placed on the cross above their head. Pilate wrote the sign that would be placed on Jesus' cross. On it, Pilate wrote: "Jesus of Nazareth, the King of the Jews." ²⁰The place where Jesus was crucified was just outside the city walls, along a main road that led in and out of the city. Many Jews read the sign's inscription, along with many others going by. Since many people passed this area, the sign was written in three different language—Aramaic, Latin, and Greek—so that everyone in the world could read it.

²¹The chief priests of the Jews objected about the sign's inscription to Pilate. "Do not leave that sign up there like that. That sign is an insult

to us. If you are going to leave it up, at least change it from 'The King of the Jews' to 'This man claimed, I am King of the Jews.'"

²²Pilate responded, "I will not change it. What I have written is what I have written."

²³When the soldiers had crucified Jesus, they took His garments and divided them up as was customary. They divided His garments into four parts, with each soldier getting a part. However, Jesus' tunic undergarment was one seamless item woven as a single piece from top to bottom. The Old Covenant Jewish people preferred seamless undergarments; they were considered a symbol of purity, and the High Priest always wore a seamless one. ²⁴The soldiers said to each other, "Let us not tear up this seamless garment. Instead, let us roll dice to see who will get it." This happened to fulfill what the Scripture says in Psalm 22:18, "They divided up My clothes among them and rolled dice for My undergarment." Little did they know, but that is why the soldiers did these things.

²⁵Standing near the cross were Jesus' mother, His mother's sister, Mary the wife of Clopas, and Mary Magdalene. ²⁶Jesus saw His mother and the disciple whom He loved standing nearby. Jesus said to His mother, "Dear woman, look, here is your new son who will take care of you."

²⁷To the disciple, Jesus said, "Look, here is your new mother that you have a responsibility to care for." From that hour on, the disciple took her into his own home and provided for her.

> 7.2.2 *Death: Jesus fulfills God's plan and dies for the world's benefit (19:28–37).*

²⁸After this, Jesus knew that all of His work had now been completed. In order to fulfill the Scripture of Psalm 69:21, Jesus said, "I am thirsty." ²⁹A jar of sour wine was nearby. So, the soldiers soaked a sponge in it, put it on a hyssop branch (the same type of branch that was used to apply the Passover lamb's blood on the door frame, the blood that saved and delivered the Israelites during the first Passover). Then, the hyssop branch—a branch that symbolizes how a perfect

Passover sacrifice's blood would save and deliver all people—was held up to Jesus' lips. ³⁰When He had received the sour wine, Jesus said, "It is finished." Then Jesus bowed His head and handed over His spirit in death; His mission had been accomplished.

³¹Jesus' crucifixion happened on the day of Preparation, the Friday before the Sabbath. The next day was a special Sabbath because, on this particular year, the Passover also occurred on the Sabbath. The Jewish leaders did not want dead bodies left on the cross during the Sabbath. So, they asked Pilate to order the legs of the crucified to be broken, which would speed up their deaths and give the soldiers time to take their bodies down before the Sabbath began.

³²The soldiers came and broke the legs of the first man crucified with Jesus; then, they broke the other man's legs. ³³But when the soldiers came to Jesus, they saw that He was already dead and that there was no need to break His legs. ³⁴Instead, to verify that He was dead, one of the soldiers pierced Jesus' side with a spear. Immediately, blood and water poured out, which indicated His heart had already stopped and that Jesus was already dead. ³⁵(The disciple writing this account saw it all. He has given an accurate report of the evidence. And his testimony is true. The disciple writing this knows he is telling you the truth about Jesus so that you may believe in Him.) ³⁶All of these things happened to fulfill the Scripture in Exodus 12:46 that says, like the perfect Lamb of God sacrificed for God's people, "Not one bone in His body will be broken." ³⁷And to fulfill another Scripture in Zechariah 12:10 that says, "They will look on the One they have pierced (for their salvation)."

7.2.3 Buried: Jesus fulfills God's plan and is buried in a tomb (19:38–42).

³⁸After Jesus had died, Joseph of Arimathea asked Pilate for permission to take down and bury Jesus' body. Joseph had been a disciple of Jesus, though a secret one because he feared repercussions from the Jewish leaders if he had been open about following Jesus. Yet he was hiding no more, asking Pilate openly for Jesus' body. Pilate permitted him. So, Joseph of Arimathea came, took Jesus' body off the cross, and

took His body away to the tomb for burial. ³⁹Nicodemus, the Jewish leader who had earlier come to visit Jesus at night, helped him with Jesus' burial. Nicodemus also brought with him a mixture of myrrh and aloes, about seventy-five pounds worth, which was an amount appropriate to honor a king. ⁴⁰In keeping with typical Jewish burial practices, these two men wrapped Jesus' body with the spices in strips of linen cloth.

⁴¹The place where they crucified Jesus was near a garden. The garden had a new tomb that had never been used before. ⁴²Since this tomb was nearby, and because it was the Jewish Day of Preparation before the Sabbath, and since the sun was about to set and the Sabbath was about to begin, the two men laid Jesus' dead body in this garden tomb.

7.3 Resurrection: Jesus, the Son of God, gives a new kind of life to the world through His resurrection (20:1–29).

> 7.3.1 The empty tomb: Jesus has risen from the dead, overcoming death, the Devil, and a world living in darkness (20:1–10).

CHAPTER 20

¹Early on Sunday morning (the first day of the week), while it was still mostly dark, Mary Magdalene came to the tomb. She saw the stone had been rolled away from tomb's entrance. ²Distraught by the scene, she ran back to Simon Peter and the other disciple, the one whom Jesus loved. She told them, "It looks like someone has taken the Lord's body out of the tomb, and we have no idea where they have put Him!"

³So, Peter and the other disciples immediately left for the tomb. ⁴Both of them were running, but the other disciple ran faster than Peter and reached the tomb first. ⁵He stuck his head into the tomb to peek inside. He noticed the linen cloths that Jesus was buried in were lying there, but he did not go inside the tomb.

⁶Then, Simon Peter arrived after the other disciple and went into the tomb. He saw the linen cloths that Jesus' body had been buried in lying there where Jesus' dead body should have been. ⁷He also noticed that the face cloth (the one that was wrapped around one's head during Jewish burials) was not lying with the other linen burial cloths. Instead, it was neatly rolled up in a different spot separate from the linen, suggesting some sort of orderly departure. ⁸Then the other disciple, the one who had reached the tomb first, went inside the tomb. When he saw what was left in the tomb, he saw purposeful intent and believed that Jesus was somehow alive.

⁹At this point, the disciples still did not understand from the Scriptures of the Old Covenant [Old Testament] that it was necessary for Jesus to rise from the dead. ¹⁰After seeing the empty tomb, the disciples went back to the house where they were staying.

> 7.3.2 *Jesus has risen from the dead, and the time is coming for Him to ascend to the Father in heaven (20:11–18).*

¹¹While the disciples had left to return to the house, Mary just stood outside the tomb crying. As she was weeping, she stuck her head to peek inside the tomb again. ¹²She saw two angels dressed in white sitting there. They were sitting on the stone bench in the burial chamber where Jesus' body had been—one where His head would have been and the other where His feet would have been.

¹³They asked Mary, "Dear woman, in this glorious moment, why are you crying?"

She said to them, "The Jewish leaders, robbers, or somebody has taken the body of my Lord away. And I do not know where they have put Him." ¹⁴After saying this, she turned around. She saw someone standing there, but she did not realize it was Jesus.

¹⁵Jesus asked her, "Dear woman, in this glorious moment, why are you crying? Who is it that you are looking for?" Unable to tell who it was that was talking to her, she assumed the person was just the gardener.

She replied, "Kind sir, if you have carried His body away, please tell me where you have put Him so that I can go and take care of His body."

¹⁶Jesus called to her, "Mary."

Then Mary turned toward Jesus and cried out in Aramaic, "Rabboni!" (which means Masterful Teacher).

¹⁷Jesus said to her, "Do not cling too tightly to My physical return in your presence. I have not yet ascended to the Father; another change, another transition, is coming. But for now, do not keep this news to yourself. Instead, go to My disciples, My spiritual brothers, and tell them that the last event of My physical time here on earth has come—that 'I am ascending to My Father and your Father, to My God and your God.'"

¹⁸Then Mary Magdalene went and told the disciples the incredible, exciting, and joyful news: "I have seen the Lord!" And she told them what Jesus had instructed her to say.

> 7.3.3 Jesus has risen from the dead, and He brings peace to His followers, gives them the Holy Spirit, and sends them out into the world to continue God's work in it (20:19–23).

¹⁹Later that evening, on the first day of the week, the disciples were gathered together behind locked doors. They were behind locked doors because they were afraid the Jewish leaders might come to arrest them and kill them too. Then, even though the doors were tightly locked, Jesus suddenly appeared among them. His physical body stood there right in front of them.

Jesus said, "May My peace—the fullness of well-being in a new kind of life with God—be with you."

²⁰After saying this, Jesus showed them His nail-scarred hands and His pierced side. His disciples were filled with an overflowing joy when they saw the Lord.

²¹Then Jesus said to them again, "May My peace be with you, for I give you the fullness of well-being in a new kind of life that calls you to live it and share it with others. As the Father has sent Me into this world with a purpose, I am sending you out into the world empowered to continue My work in it."

²²After Jesus said this, He breathed on them and said, "Receive the Holy Spirit. ²³Having received the Holy Spirit and being led by Him, if you forgive anyone's sins, they are forgiven. Likewise, if you do not forgive anyone's sins, they are not forgiven."

> 7.3.4 Jesus has risen from the dead, and He provides Thomas with the physical evidence of His resurrection so that he will believe; yet, Jesus says that those who believe without seeing Him physically are supernaturally blessed by God (20:24-29).

²⁴When Jesus first appeared to the disciples, Thomas (nicknamed Didymus, which meant the Twin), who was one of Jesus's inner circle of twelve disciples, was not with them. ²⁵The other disciples told Thomas what had happened. They said to him, "With our own eyes, we have seen the risen Lord!"

But Thomas doubted. Thomas told them, "I will not believe it unless I see it for myself. Unless I see the nail marks in His hands, and unless I can put my fingers on the place where the nails went, and unless I can put my hand into His side, I will not believe."

²⁶Eight days later, the disciples were gathered together in the same house once again, and Thomas was with them this time. Even though the doors were locked shut, Jesus appeared and physically stood in front of them. He said, "May My peace—the fullness of well-being in a new kind of life with God—be with you."

²⁷Then Jesus said to Thomas, "Put your finger here and inspect My nailed-scared hands. Reach out your hand and put it into My pierced side. Stop doubting and believe."

²⁸Thomas responded to Jesus, "I realize fully that You are My Lord and My God! I believe."

²⁹Jesus said to him, "Because you have seen Me resurrected in a physical body, you have believed. But what divine and supernatural favor rests on those have who have not seen Me physically and yet have believed."

8. The Purpose of John's Gospel: Believe in Jesus and continue to believe in Him (20:30–31).

³⁰The resurrected Jesus did many other signs that revealed deeper truths about God in the presence of His disciples, but they are not written in this book. ³¹But these things are written in this book so that you may believe—and keep on believing—that Jesus is the Christ, the Son of God who saves the world. These things were written so that by trusting in Jesus, you may have a new kind of life—one that provides transformation now and that eternally endures—in His name.

9. The Conclusion of the Gospel of John: Believers will continue to live by faith in the resurrected Christ and continue His work in the world (21:1–25).

9.1 Even after the resurrection, Jesus provides for His followers and continues His work in the world through them (21:1–14).

CHAPTER 21

¹Some time after this, Jesus appeared again to His disciples. They were at the Sea of Tiberias (which is also known as the Sea of Galilee). ²Gathered together there were Simon Peter, Thomas (also nicknamed Didymus, which means the Twin), Nathanael from Cana in Galilee,

the two sons of Zebedee, and two other disciples. ³Then Simon Peter said to them, "I am going fishing."

They replied, "We will go fishing with you." So, they went out and got in the boat. They fished all night and caught nothing.

⁴Just as the morning light began to replace the night's darkness, Jesus was standing on the shore. However, these disciples did not recognize that it was Jesus.

⁵Jesus called out to them from the shore, "Friends, how did the fishing go? Did you catch any fish?"

They replied, "No. We have had our trammel nets dropped into the water and spread between two boats (which would have built vertical walls around any fish). And we have cast our nets into the water so that they could fall down and catch the fish. But after fishing like this all night, we caught nothing."

⁶Jesus said to them, "Do not worry about the trammel nets. Just throw your cast net over the other side of the boat (the open right side), and you will find some fish." Without the trammel nets set to wall the fish in, this was basically just a long shot and a random throw of the net into the water. But they figured it was worth a try. When they cast the net, they captured such a large number of fish that the weight was too much for them to haul onto the boat.

⁷The disciple whom Jesus loved said to Peter, "It is the Lord!" When Simon Peter realized that it was the Lord, he wrapped his outer garment around himself (since he had minimal clothing on while fishing) and jumped into the water to swim to shore. ⁸The other disciples followed behind him in the boats. Since they were only about 100 yards from land, they dragged the net full of fish through the water to shore. ⁹When they landed, they saw a charcoal fire already burning. It already had some fish cooking on it, along with some bread.

¹⁰Jesus said to them, "Bring some of the fish that you have just caught over here with you."

¹¹So Simon Peter climbed on the boat, helping them haul the net ashore. The net was full, having 153 largre fish in it, and yet it was not torn.

¹²Jesus said to them, "Come and have some breakfast." They did not need to ask Him, "Who are you?" because they fully recognized Him. They knew with certainty that is was Jesus. ¹³Then Jesus came and took the bread and gave it to them. He did the same with the fish—fully sharing a meal with them.

¹⁴This was now the third time that Jesus had appeared to His disciples after He was raised from the dead.

9.2 Believers may come short of what God wants for them, but Jesus restores them, and He refocuses them so that they can carry on His continuing work in the world (21:15–23).

¹⁵After they had finished breakfast, Jesus said to Simon Peter, "Simon, son of John, you said you would always be faithful to Me, even if the others deserted Me. So, let Me ask you, do you love Me more than these others?"

He said, "Yes, Lord; You know that I love You."

Jesus replied, "Then I have important work for you to do—feed My lambs."

¹⁶Jesus said to him a second time, "Simon Peter, son of John, do you love Me?"

He said, "Yes, Lord; You know that I love You."

Jesus replied, "Then I have important work for you to do—take care of My sheep."

¹⁷Jesus said to him a third time, "Simon Peter, son of John, do you love Me?"

Recalling how he had denied Jesus three times, Peter was grieved that Jesus had asked Him the same question—"Do you love Me?"—three times. Peter answered, "Lord, You know all things. You know that I love You."

Jesus replied, "Then I have important work for you to do—feed My sheep. [18]Also, let Me tell you this important truth: When you were young, you had a lot of freedom. You were not restrained and walked wherever you wanted. But when you are old, you will stretch out your hands, like on a cross, and someone else will restrain you—binding and fastening you down—and lead you where you do not want to go."

[19]Jesus was telling Peter this to indicate what kind of death he would die and how it would show God's all-surpassing value and worth to the world. Then Jesus said to Peter, "Follow Me."

[20]Peter turned and saw that the disciple whom Jesus loved was following behind them. This was the same disciple who had leaned back against Jesus at the Last Supper and asked, "Lord, who is it that is going to betray You?"

[21]When Peter saw him, he asked Jesus, "Lord, what about this man? What is going to happen to him?"

[22]Jesus replied, "If I want him to remain alive until I come again, what does that matter to you? Each person has their own unique purpose in life, yet all are called to one common thing—to follow Me. Rather than worrying about what will happen to someone else, you should focus on one thing: Following Me."

[23]Because of this saying by Jesus, the rumor spread among the believers that this disciple would not die but remain until Jesus returned from heaven. But Jesus did not say that the disciple would not die. Jesus was not being literal but using hyperbole when He said, "If I want him to remain alive until I come again, what does that matter to you?"

9.3 Much more could be said, but believers have this official, eye-witness account to encourage their belief in the truth of God revealed in Jesus Christ (21:24–25).

²⁴The disciple they were talking about is the same one who is sharing this account, giving his eyewitness testimony to the reality of all these things, and who has now written them down here to preserve an official record about Jesus. We know and have verified that his testimony is true.

²⁵Beyond what is recorded here, there are so many other things that Jesus did. If they were all written down, I suppose that the whole world would not be big enough to contain all the books that would be written about who He is and what He has done.

www.ingramcontent.com/pod-product-compliance
Lightning Source LLC
Chambersburg PA
CBHW070738020526
44118CB00035B/1521